Ceremonies of Life, Rituals of Death

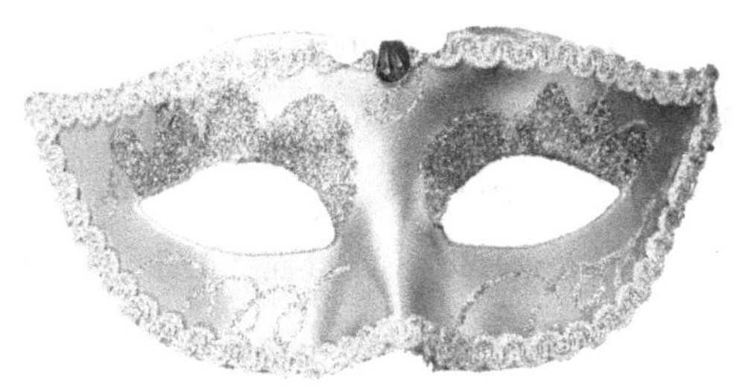

Daniel Vidart

Contents

INTRODUCTION

In the pages of this book there coexist, united in the hermeneutic attempt of a single interpreter and expressed in the personal style of an intimate writer, representative of the currently not very recommendable quality of polygrapher, or polymath, which is even more archaizing and less appreciated, three different treatments of a theme that crosses, as a stubborn constant, the history of the human species.

This theme refers to a coin, the most common and worn coin in the Universe, which rolls from hand to hand and from millennium to millennium on the folder of the existential tapestry.

On the obverse side of that coin flies the chubby cherub of life and on the reverse side walks, with a slow and sure step, the skull of death.

The complementary univocality of both faces, the smiling and the stark, death also smiles in its own way, shows the ancestral and reciprocal relationship that confronts them and at the same time corroborates them. That is why men wonder if this pairing is a *conditio sine qua non* of the shared meaning of both, which are defined and explained one in function of the other, or if this tension, dialogic rather than dialectic, which unites them and at the same time separates them, is a free gift of cosmic chance or a planned strategy of Providence.

For their part, the three announced treatments of the subject appeal to the literary-philosophical or essayistic mode, to the (seductive) epistemological rigor of the natural sciences, and, finally, to the systemic vision currently adopted by the anthropo-social disciplines, respectively.

The title of the book does not do justice to the range of issues outlined in its pages. Nor have these serious and urgent issues been deeply investigated, if indeed a thorough analysis of the last scene of things can be practiced. But the title points, perhaps as a lure–as a way to help the editor- to the extremes of the dispute between euthanasia, considered from an ethnological point of view, at the level of the traditional practices of the peoples, on the one hand, and the technology of the I.C.U., a wonder of contemporary scientific knowledge and know-how to do contemporary scientists, on the other.

I warn that I am not against the remarkable help that this "state-of-the-art" medical tool can provide in the rescue or preservation of life in cases where its use is fully justified. But I protest against the arrogance of a biocracy, which in the end becomes a thanatocracy, whose theory and practice appeal to pride rather than philanthropy. In this way, and with scandal, I condemn the use of I.C.U., when the artificial prolongation of existence does not concern the will of the patient, already evicted, but the will of a team of specialists who - allied, rather with the Devil than with God - undertake the adventure of prolonging physiologically considered life, to the detriment of the soul and spirit of the patient, already obscured, or suddenly illuminated, by the dawn of death.

The inclusion of a chapter about the carnival in a theme on advent and ultimacy may also come as a surprise. But the thing is that at the crossroads of the carnival festival, almost since prehistoric times, the ceremonies of life that are always reborn - the little horses, the bears, the sprinkling of water, the fornication that accompanies the masquerades - and the symbols of death, always efficient and ubiquitous, converge: the snow-white little masks of "a vintén", the faces painted white, the games with flour that, by whitening the bodies, pamper the warmth of the corpses - and, complementarily, evoke the grace of the bread that sustains life - or the paleness of Pierrot, who copies the lunar physiognomy of the deceased, since after all, he is a dead man suddenly thrust into the Venetian ballrooms and on the stages of the *Commediadell'Arte*.

It is true that the carnival in our days is very far from its primitive expression, many of which survived until the forties in the city of Montevideo. Fallen in the hands of the civilization of consumption, which commercialize them and move them away from the collective rituals of the people, the old Shrovetide disappear or become dysfunctional, as it happens with the intolerable televised stupidity of the "llamadas", turned from sound relics of a chilling ritual drama as they were once, into a vedettes and transvestites dance.

The nowadays parades of the troupe of blacks, and not lubolos, as it is erroneously said as taking the part for the whole, without those formidable strings of drums, which made the hair stand up on the back of the neck and make everyone, actors and spectators, fall into a trance, have lost, along with their creative spontaneity, the shamanic clattering of the virtuous drummers of yesterday. It is no longer a rhythmic tempest, hallucinating and sweeping at the same time, born at the folkloric bonfires, where instead of just slices of it, the cosmic forces as powers of nature were tempered, but a spectacle for tourists and viewers whose deep essence never belonged to the popularly said carnival, the workmanship of the Faustian West, but tribal ritualism, a symbol of magical Africa.

The general lack of knowledge of the ethnic and historical background of carnival requires an anthropological tracing of its phenomenology. If this research is carried out according to adequate methodological standards, its results will undoubtedly surprise many. Unsuspected roots will then be discovered in a ceremony where, Afterlife the paraphernalia displayed by the comparsas and murgas [traditional folk music and dance performers], life and death, closely intertwined, make their periodic encounter in an upside-down world.

Before closing this personal presentation of the six chapters that make up the book, in which philosophy, ritual, myth, and religion are in dialogue, I would like to point out that the first of them is devoted to a strictly scientific topic. In that chapter, I refer to the treatment that biologists give to the phenomenon of life, considering in what ways they define it and what characteristics they attribute to it. From this backdrop, other types of visions, alien to the scientific approach to reality, will be cut out. This contrast will serve to reveal the incompleteness of a style of knowledge applied to the so-called rational explanation of things, as proposed by science, the seductive conjurer of the errors and horrors of archaic witchcraft, traditional healers, indigenous botany, and the therapeutic ravings of those addicted to peyote or ayahuasca.

By mentioning the word science, academics take for granted that in order to board their spaceship, the puerility of myth, the dogma of religion, and the mirages of metaphysics have been left behind, abandoned on a misty shore of the planet of the apes. This is what Comte proclaimed in the last century, inaugurating the third and definitive stage, the positive one, corresponding to a "true" conception, that is, definitive and unshakable, of the world around. What it happens is that in the psychic infrastructure of the scientists - seat of the labyrinths of the unconscious, the myopias of prejudice and the prestidigitation of ideologies - echoes resound the anguished interrogations and the stammering answers that this issue, life, and death, death and life, has unleashed in the souls of men. The reason why the much demanded and offered objectivity is impossible. Firstly, the usual procedures of science do not guarantee absolute truth and knowledge because they have been established by an entity vitiated by inaccuracy and error, which is the human being himself. Secondly, if there really were an objective science applied to the infallible deciphering of reality, parti-pris, ethnocentrism, prejudice and the vested interests of the scientists themselves would cancel the assurances of absolute objectivity.

Every man is committed to a vision of the world, prior to the practice of science, art, or any community activity. Each person contemplates the social and natural environment through the lenses of his personal subjectivity, which is shaped, strangely enough, by the gravitation of the dominant culture. The popular saying was able to capture this characteristic when it expressed that "things have the color of the glass through which they are seen".

To clarify the first point, related to the fallibility of the sciences, it should be remembered that these epistemic disciplines harbor in their bosom, and in spite of the Academy, a group of annoying heterodox who denounce the sloppiness of the inductive processes and the mental characteristics of the human observer, equally afflicted by error and incompleteness.

These devil's advocates, sometimes malgré-eux, continually question the sanctity and infallibility of the scientific law, of the absolute equation, of the incontrovertible theorem. Einstein and those who alerted the unconditional believers about the proven fallibility of official science - Popper, Black, Cohen, Peirce, etc. - constituted, after all, a herd of unwelcome black sheep in the herd of the faithful of a new church invented on the ruins of the other, that of superstition, dogma, and miracle. In this sense, that extraordinary genius, who very late learned higher mathematics and whose theory of relativity was at first a poietic act, a metaphor of intelligence, issued a warning that should appear in the heading of all texts of "normal science", that is, those written in the light of the paradigms in use, according to Kuhn's terminology.

Einstein wrote: «Since perception only directly informs us of this external world or physical reality, we can only grasp the latter by speculative means and therefore, our notions about physical reality can never be definite. We must always be prepared to modify these notions - that is, the axiomatic structure of physics - in order to do justice in the most logically perfect way to the facts received. Indeed, a glance at the development of physics is enough to convince us that it has undergone far-reaching modifications in the course of time»

Having said this, it is now time to stop. The prologue, which in reality is always an epilogue, has already exhausted its subject matter. Let the reader then prepare themselves to enter into the controversial substance of this book, which, given that is crepuscular, has, for me, the value of a testament. Through my long, already prolonged residence on Earth, I have, more than once, felt the soft touch of the wings of the angel of death. The reason why I have embraced life and lived it, child of error and contingency, fallible and sinful creature, always discovering in it dazzling plenitudes and recognizing the intimate failures that prevented me from preserving them, rediscovering them, or renewing them. This has been happening over the course of many decades at the dictation of the ups and downs which alternate joys and misfortunes, and vice versa. In this way I have learned that one should not hurry or shy away from the hour of truth, that is to say, the last hour, which will come when the ropes of the swing break.

I thank Claudio Rama - whom I have known and loved since the beautiful days when, as a full-time child, played with my children at the intersection of Timbó and Zubillaga streets, in a perpetual and bustling coming and going between my house and the house of Ángel, his father, of whom many years later, he and I accompanied, with so many other mourners, to his grave in the good land of Bogotá - for having encouraged me to put together these papers and for his generous willingness to publish them. Now, I have nothing more to tell you, my potential readers. This book, from this moment on, has begun its own life, which runs separately from mine. May it have the strength to be passed on, walking from hand to hand and from spirit to spirit, to editorially multiply, a goal that is the ambition of every author and, more than anything else, to transmit the stories that it keeps in its pages and carries on its shoulder, humbly and with restraint.

THE BIOLOGISTS AND LIFE

Throughout time, multiple philosophical, scientific, and theological conceptions have emerged about what life is (and is not)[1]. Science current achievements allow us to order, operationally, although not definitively, a series of definitions. Some descriptive, others explanatory; those are analytical, these are systemic. All of them, nevertheless, suffer from incompleteness, all are affected by partiality, all show the here and now of epistemic paradigms and the present state of scientific ideologies.

Life can be defined, to begin with, as an entity arising from the interrelation of water with carbohydrates, gradads, proteins, and nucleic acids. Regarding the latter, Riley states that "if there is indeed a real difference and dividing line between living and inanimate things, it must lie in the domain of viruses and nucleic acids"[2].

If we go through a biology text from the beginning of the century, after telling us that life is the set of phenomena that oppose death, with which very little progress is made in

---

[1] I select, among a torrential bibliography, a few accessible books: E. Schrödinger, *¿Qué es la vida?* Espasa-Calpe Argentina, Buenos Aires, 1947; C. U. M. Smith, **El problema de la vida**. Alianza, Madrid, 1977; F. Jacob, **La lógica de lo viviente**. Laia, Barcelona, 1963; S. E. Luria, **La vida, experimento inacabado**. Alianza, Madrid, 1975

[2] J. F. Riley, **Introducción a la biología.** Alianza, Madrid, 1970

the positive characterization of the former, the author, like the other treatises of his time, then resorts to a concept which is subject to the limitations of the physiological vision: a living being feeds, metabolizes, excretes, breathes, grows, reproduces, reacts to environmental stimuli, moves, etc..., even though almost all plants and many animals do not move, anaerobic bacteria do not breathe and viruses limit themselves to reproducing at the expense of a unicellular host, a fact that was not yet known.

Further forward, during the intense developments in research that marked the decades from the 1920s to the 1940s, the spectacular progress in genetics, in parallel with the renovation, deepening, and complementation of the theories of Lamarck, Darwin-Wallace, and De Vries, made it possible to characterize living beings as systems capable of evolving through the processes of natural selection. The first figures of research were the flies of the genus Drosophila. From that point, chromosomes, genes, and the processes of mitosis (division of chromosomes into two halves) and meiosis (halving of the number of chromosomes) were incorporated into the biological language and to the explanation of the mechanisms of inheritance.

During the last half of the twentieth century, considered the generator of a colossal biological revolution, the definitions of life were enriched by two new points of view: that of molecular biology and that of Energetics, which can also be named as the field covered by Thermodynamics, an old-fashioned denomination that should be discarded.

Molecular biology, concentrating its attention on the genetic code, contemplates living beings as systems whose hereditary information, complex and neatly encoded in the helical chains of nucleic acids, is reproduced in and by their descendants. At the same time, these beings have the property of regulating their metabolism, i.e. their exchanges of matter and energy with the environment, due to the action of certain modifiers of the rate of molecular reactions. These protein catalysts are called enzymes, i.e. soluble ferments, as indicated by their Greek etymology. Chemistry takes the place of physiology, which after all is nothing more than the physics of the organism, in the in-depth study of metabolic and genetic processes.

The definition of living beings, according to the energetic, in consequence, establishes that a living being constitutes an open system whose internal processes of retroaction cause the decreasing of entropy through the functioning of a homeostatic regulating plate, even if this means an increase in entropy in the surrounding environment. The neguentropy of the organism accelerates the entropy of the surrounding environmental systems. This is a fundamental principle to be taken into account. Life was defined by Bergson as the struggle against entropy, but life entropy around it. This is how Hladik has seen it; he states that the establishment of biotic order does not necessarily correspond to a local decrease in entropy: "an increase in entropy may then be compatible with the creation of a certain order"[3].

Taking into account all the above contributions, contemporary science has settled on a provisional systemic definition, namely: "a living being is an open system that organizes at the expense of the entropy increase of the external environment with which it carries out, through a certain number of processes, exchanges of matter and energy governed by codes that it can transmit to its heirs and that is perfected through natural selection"[4]

---

[3] H. Hladik, **La biofísica.** Fondo de la Cultura Económica, México, 1982.

[4] C. Arnau, J. Cabo, **El origen de la vida.** Salvat, Barcelona, 1977

In current conceptualizations of life, there is a kind of self-absorption on the cell, to the detriment of the role of the organism or the systemic approach to communities of living beings. In order to generate a broader vision, which attends respectively and concomitantly to the thing and its surrounding - circumstance, we must start from another point of view. Without the energy of the Sun, life would not be possible. Nor would it be possible without the existence of a great quantity of water, and this was noticed very early by the thinkers of the East and the West: water is the *arjé*, the essential Apeiron that originates living beings. Finally, there is a third factor: life cannot take place without the existence of interfaces between the liquid, solid and gaseous states of matter on the surface of the globe.

In the chinks of these interfaces, materials move, elements shift, cyclic rounds of atoms and molecules ascend and descend. But everything happens in a dialectical relationship with life itself. Millions and millions of tons of minerals are mobilized, shifted, processed, in short, by the planetary biomass. This matter, requested and expelled according to pre-fixed rhythms, enters and leaves the biotic systems. In living beings, two elements are sovereign: oxygen intervenes in around 65% to 70% and hydrogen in around 10%. The remainder, around 20% to 25%, is made up of a set of more than 70 elements in which carbon, nitrogen, phosphorus, sulfur, sodium, potassium, calcium, magnesium, cobalt, copper, zinc, and chlorine predominate. Carbon, a major player in the organization of matter thanks to its linkages and bonds, plays a fundamental role, despite its lesser abundance, which should be especially emphasized.

In a less relevant group are aluminum, boron, bromine, iodine, selenium, chromium, molybdenum, vanadium, silicon, strontium, barium, nickel, and cadmium, which are responsible for assisting in specific functions or acting in specific organs. Sometimes, the lack of a trace element becomes a life-limiting factor, as Liebig understood by studying the development of plants in various types of soils.

The list of elements is longer than the specified, but life does not arise from the sum or mixture of these simple elements. The atoms that generate the aforementioned elements, on the other hand, are present in all the recycles imposed by biotization on the surface of the Earth.

One more condition: for life to be possible, these elements must come together in compatible clusters and not at random, under certain given conditions. It is, therefore, necessary to start from the molecules, from the stable electronic bonds between the elements so that life can find a base, in order to establish an adequate structure and functionality on it. Any person who believes that God's finger snap is indispensable has every right to presuppose his existence for life to emerge. Of course, it should not be forgotten the first cosmic Creation, in which perhaps, as Teilhard de Chardin maintained, all the seeds that later germinated have been given, as crouched and in an underlying larval state: life, man, the soul, and the spirit of reasoning and feeling noosphere.

Biological systems are composed of certain molecular matrix combinations. One of them, I repeat, is water, which is generally cited as if it were not in common usage. Our organism, which seems so solid, is 70% water: human beings are after all mere bags covered by an epidermis that keep the liquid legacy of the primordial sea. Jellyfish are almost "living waters" as the popular lexicon says: they harbor 95% water in their transparent corporeality. The molecular entities that command the biotic vessel are also made up of carbohydrates, fats, and proteins, to which, sine qua non, nucleic acids must be added. Carbohydrates, sugar, starch, glycogen, among others, are formed from the combination of water and carbon.

However, the molecular background is composed of oxygen, hydrogen, and carbon. Fats and lipids have more carbon and hydrogen than sugars and they burn slowly, which transforms them into useful fuel reserves for every organism. Proteins add nitrogen to the previous trio of elements. These large molecules, animators of living systems, are composed of amino acids, minor but no fewer essential molecules.

Much remains to be said about vital phenomena. Life is one and diverse: it constitutes a *continuum*, and is pulverized in species whose biodiversity - long live the difference! - adapts the beings that integrate it to the most diverse environments while projecting themselves in them or modifying them tenaciously and permanently; life is, therefore, both protean and plastic at the same time. This plasticity derives from the presence of carbon as a leading agent in living systems and from the permanence and consistency of water, which makes up 75% of plants and 60% of animals. The water dissolves, inhibits, transports, composes, and circulates. In 95% of the living matter, the subtle processes of molecular alchemy, which are built with oxygen, carbon, hydrogen, and nitrogen, are mobilized in water. When adding to this quartet an octet of other elements, according to the order already indicated, 99.99% of the total is obtained. Therefore, biochemistry and not biophysics is the science that must study the molecular basis of life.

Current neuroendocrinology has put an end to the physicalism of neuro-electricity. After the discovery of the enzymatic role of permeases, osmosis is no longer considered a mere physical process. The metabolism imposes a *crescendo* which, starting from the homeostasis regulated by the reactions taking place inside the cell, is installed, level after level, in all the retroacting systems of the organism and in the hierarchical structure of animal and plant species. Life is labile, it adapts like a rule of Lesbos to environmental irregularities, but it does not do so with a kaleidoscopic repertoire of a few repeated strategies but through a continuous innovating mode. Life is, as Crusafont Pairó says, a self-inventor. "The evolution of living beings... is nothing more than a formidable procession of self-inventions, for, with and through them, to conquer the planet they parasitize. Thus, making a quick summary, the invention, already indicated, of sexual reproduction, much more economical in the negentropic race of life than simple bipartition and pedogamy; the invention of autotrophy, in contrast to heterotrophy, and with it, this essential dichotomy between the two kingdoms: plant and animal, starting from the viral; the invention of the solidarity represented by the metazoans, in whose primordial formula we already find a mimic or a first essay of morula; the invention of mesenchyme in the Sponges, mesenchyme that will be even more important in the higher vertebrates and in man himself; the attempts at the invention of the celoma, when the struggle between the autonomy of the jellyfish and the dependence of the polyps is debated; the invention of the organization of hierarchical work in the Syphonophora, a prelude to the lineage that we will find in social insects; the invention of the power of regeneration, not entirely lost even in vertebrates, where the embryo of the newt can be fragmented and each of the parts regenerates the whole. Max de Ceccaty [the author who inspires this development of Crusafont Pairó] expresses <that, after the spectacular demonstrations> that we have just seen, will come the time of <the clandestine revolutions>, when passing from the aquatic life, i.e., from what we would call neologically, the homeoecia or more or less marked constancy of the medium in which the organisms were bathed, to terrestrial life, to the animals take, to their interior, <the oceanic medium> and try and invent, by multiple ways, the progressive homeostasis. ... thanks to the invention of a circulatory system and of a blood curiously constructed under a chemical scheme so similar to the one from worms to man. We proceed to other interior revolutions until we reach the brain of the crania or vertebrates, in which the stimulus-integrating to psycho-integrating systems is invented, starting from the purely tropho-integrating ones of the inferior beings"[5].

Life, finally, is efficient without waste; it uses optimizing means in the performance and minimizing ones in the effort. It tries to plot, apart from the imperatives of the environment, an inner organization that affirms its own selfhood while expanding the projection of its physiology towards the immediate environment. That is to say, the internal environment seeks to preserve the economy and rationality of its system by taking it outward, if one can say so, prolonging it in the external environment in order to defend its neurotropic capacity even at the cost of sowing entropy in the surrounding environment.

According to Claude Bernard's expression, the permanence of the internal environment, in constant struggle with the oscillations and aggressions of the external environment, constitutes "the very condition of freedom". This freedom is assured in the systems of living beings that have achieved a position of privilege in the evolutionary chain, as it results from the organism-environment dialectic, according to the quantity and quality of the information in the different vital systems.

Thus, and already invading the field of metaphysics, the famous French physiologist believes that life, a perpetual creation exercised by the dynamics of survival in charge of the metabolism of animals and plants, express its *raison d'être* in the activity of "the creative and organizing force of the organism". Faced with so much certainty, which in the end gets

---

[5] M. Crusafont Pairó, **El fenómeno vital.** Labor, Barcelona, 1967.

18

bogged down in an evasive gibberish, in a saying that says nothing, Rostand, another contemporary French biologist, avails himself of the benefits of doubt: "I do not know what life is, nor consciousness, nor thought". And we are still there, both the ignorant, among whom I include myself and the few true sages of this world.

FOR AN ETHNOLOGY OF DEATH

In the world of western societies where the civilization of consumption reigns, the theme of death and the occurrence of death are separated. War and social violence multiply and make the sudden irruption of death a daily occurrence, augmented by the disastrous harvests of illness and expiration, but what the TV man contemplates is the illustrated obituary of caricature-like ghosts, of theatrical protagonists whose cycle begins and ends on the screen of an electronic device: in real life death, does not seem to exist and is not even thought of. The demystification hedonism of *carpe diem* invites us to enjoy the propitious, to dress the shiny new object with the finery of instantaneousness, to comply with the demands of a youthful axiology that dictates the tone of life, to not be ashamed of the *Weltanschauung*novel that mediatizes the Being in the name of Having.

Those who die are the others; they are the former owners of the bodies that appear in the photographic or film imagery where, in pêle-mêle, appear the bombed Iraqis, the assassinated social activists, the executed street children, the old people run over by cars, the tourists burned in aviation catastrophes. Thus, death is subjected to a series of systematic prestidigitation: there is no more talk about The Lady or The Damned that overwhelmed souls during the centuries of "barbarism" and, in order to decisively remove the arena of the living from any contamination with the funerary proceedings, the home funerals disappear to the spell of the office etiquette of a company that replaces the pathetic, mournful and smelly scene of family mourning with an air-conditioned room. And above all, as the ultimate concealment of the lethal outcome imposed by illness or accident, the dying patients are confined, segregated, and condemned to the desert of their solitary agony. As domestic agony and dying scandalize, the resources of concealment are used, that is, hospital confinement, either in its popular version or in its luxury packaging. There, from the collective overcrowded room or the rumbustious suite, the aliens rejected by the living who avoid death and its procession of allusions or anticipations will be subjected, when the patient gets worse, regardless of age or inviability, to the discreet internment in the I.C.U. This laboratory of occultism, resuscitated salamanca of demonic knowledge, guarantees the good purposes of a science, perhaps without much conscience, allied with a more and more subtle and powerful technique. The seriously ill person, who was taken from his home bed and separated from his family and friends, is finally handed over to the bureaucracy of death. In this way, he is sometimes turned into a commodity and always into a procedure, a password, a therapeutic or surgical file.

Considering this, the realities of our merciless 20th-century planet, the sun of life, according to the narcissistic symbology of postmodernism, is never hidden or, at most, it rolls over the horizon as it does in the high circumpolar latitudes. Death is transformed in such a way thanks to that midnight sun, in a half-dawn, half-twilight gloom. Installed in the crack of a singular slumber, death and life converse quietly in a calm dialogue with no shocks or drama. Those who are on the sidelines of this extreme colloquy are not aware, nor do they want to be aware, of its vicissitudes. This existential detachment defines above all things the spirit, apparently frivolous, but in reality the son of the Great Fear, typical of our times.

We, city dwellers of the millennium that is coming to an end, want to forget about death, but, as María Elena Walsh says in a youthful poem, "what happens is that she [death] does not forget". The same does not happen with the peasants or with the (wrongly) called "primitive contemporaries". In the same way, the cultures of the traditionalist West -this is folk-loric- prior to the Industrial Revolution, contemplated death as a blessed term and not as a catastrophe or a curse. Nowadays, the pre-literate tribes and the Third World communities of the countryside and the slums surrounding the big cities have not been able to escape, as the secularized urban dwellers claim to have done, neither from the trembling of the Cosmos nor from the fear of the whim of the gods. In these contemporary worlds, although not contemporary with that of merchants and technologists, death goes hand in hand with life, it sits at the table with propitiatory dinners; accompanies walkers and sleepers, converses with the elderly, and plays with children.

LIMITS FOR AN INFINITE DISCOURSE

To die in the heart of the civilization of waste, justified by the hedonistic philosophies that underline the pragmatism of the executives, and to die in the theological European Middle Ages or in the mythical territory of the illiterate, supposes an identical act from the physiological point of view. But this event, an earthquake in the souls that remain and a liberation in the souls that leave, refracts with very different spectra when subjected to the test of the cultural prism. This justifies, on the scientific level, the systematization of an anthropology of death from an ethnography and an ethnology of a phenomenon consubstantial to the destiny of our species.

The rock disintegrates, the plant and the animal perish: the only man dies insofar as he anticipates death and carries it nailed to his life, either as an anguish present at all times or as a tabooed but no less implacable finitude.

Death is only one in the human condition, it is multiple in the rituals that the variables of the uses and customs, prevailing in historical societies, impose on the moments that precede or precede it.

Timor mortis conturbat me: so, says and repeats over and over again the somber refrain in Latin that is reiterated throughout the hundred verses on the transience of life with which the Scottish poet William Dunbar (1460 - 1520) deplores the mowing down of his confreres: (look for the poem in English and check)

> *He has Blind Harry and Sandy*
> *Traill Slain with his schour of mortal hail,*
> *Quhilk Patrick Johnstoun might nought flee*

The *Lament for the Makeris* (the makers, the creators, the poets, in short) expresses the feelings and thoughts of a time in which popular Christianity, victim of famine, of the Black Death, of widespread ignorance and of the iron gauntlet of the feudal barons, sought in another realm what it could not find in this valley of tears:

> *Our earthly pleasure is all vainglory;*
> *this false world is but transitory,*
> *the flesh is weak and the Enemy crafty.*

In the same way, François Villon and Jorge Manrique condoled as much for *"les dames du tempsjadi"* as for the *"infantes de Aragon"*, whose steps on earth were like the *"dews of the meadows"*. Death took the great and the small in the same raid, and all greenery perished before its unerring aim:

> *When you come in anger*
> *you make everything clear*
> *with your arrow.*

This elegiac accent, common to Christian Europe, echoes like a touch of the dead in the eschatological hemisphere of the Middle Ages, neither so average nor so dark that it did not have in the other, that of the brief life, an explosive charge of smiling and licentious plenitude. Thus, lived and enjoyed the tavern and jocund people that formed the Corte de los Milagros and the florid caterpillar of the vivid, the rogues, the sopistas, the bachilleres, the goliards, the beggars and other roadrunners that Hesse, the writer, with *Narcissus and*

Goldmund, and Orff, the musician, with *Carmina Burana*, knew how to exhume from their centenary picaresque niches.

In any case, despite this contradiction between ascetic renunciation and worldly debauchery, one cannot deny the shrunken existence of the Middle Ages, which was shaken by the *memento mori* of singular persons and by the *moriendi* arts of unnamed image-makers who depicted in their terrifying illustrations the struggle between angels and demons fighting over the dying man's wing. The Middle Ages, after the slaughter imposed by the Black Death, was characterized by the imagery of the Dances of Death, a funereal motif that has been revived over and over again in the history of literature and art.

The public and private terror for the hour of death and for what lies before and after it, that is to say, the agony of the body and the destiny of the soul constitutes a constant in all cultures and civilizations old or contemporary, that is, lateral, to our era of shiny plastic and the sporting exaltation of sex, skill, and strength. Before and after the *pulviseriset in pulvisreverteris* of the biblical Genesis, the meditation on the fleetingness of life and its ineluctable end, full of questions, accompanies and shapes the destiny of men. Anguish for me, anguish for you, and anguish for us: behind the dialectic of affective solidarity unfolds a whole melancholic repertoire of physical or metaphysical considerations on the embodied person that crosses like a shooting star the firmament of a humanity that, in order to survive as a mass, as a species, as a biotic and cultural collective, ceaselessly kills and replenishes its members as individuals.

THE ABSENT DEATH: GOLDEN AGES, PARADISES....

In the mythical Golden Ages, death did not exist or, at most, as Hesiod says, "one died as one sleeps". On the other hand, in the Judeo-Christian civilization, in the Garden of Paradise - in Persian *pairidaeza*, which in Greek became *paradeisos*, meaning garden or enclosed park, that is, the *hortusconclusus* of the latins - the initial couple Adam-Eve tastes the fruit of the Tree of Wisdom, which already supposes sin, and after it, the entrance of the domains of death. The innocents who populate the earthly paradises invented by the gods do not die because they do not actually live. Life is stalking, action, astonishment, and disenchantment at the same time, critical and vigilant conscience, random gnoseology, and a struggle with otherness. When the first couple begins to live humanly, to know, it does not do so on its own initiative, but tempted by the Devil, the *Diabolos*, the one who sows discord, the one who separates, either with the unholy light of the *logos* that is born of the *parxis*, or with the analytical arguments, and therefore dissociating, of reason. Eating from this fruit brings with it knowledge but also death. God, the Great Unity, the Creator of Heaven, the Demiurge of the Earth and its ecosystems, the Father of man (that humble being who humbles himself before his greatness, who sinks his forehead in the humus before the majestic rumor of his passing) reluctantly tolerated that his human creatures should know Good and Evil, and perhaps sighed with relief when he realized that disobedience provoked by evil temptation would turn them into inevitable prey to death. That is why, by expelling sinners from Paradise, he definitively prevented them from eating the scandalous fruit of the other forbidden tree, the Tree of Life: wise or knowledgeable, yes; immortal, and therefore identical to the gods, never.

Human wisdom and sapience become in such a way the supreme joke of the Creator: they will only be wisdom and sapience of death. The ultimate knowledge of man is, paradoxically, the knowledge that he will die.

The disdainful savage, that is, the one who lives in the jungles - *Selvagem* is a Portuguese toponym that other languages have loaded with unfavorable value judgments - and not the brute or the ruthless, as Eurocentric ideology demands, reflects, as do the civilized, on the expiration of individual life. His expressive avenues differ from ours but aim at an identical target of dread and shudder. In the metaphors of myth and in the manipulations of magic, the predecessor of science for it handles like the latter the relations between cause and effect, there is an intuitive version of things and processes, of what remains and what continues, of the unique and the multiple. A grammar of the world is then constructed and it is one that we must decode scientifically, --*emicversusetic*-- instead of continuing to proclaim with a pertinacity that anguish is a privilege of the literate cultures of the West.

The Brave and the Lazy

A poem by the *Crow* redskins, early swept away by the genocide consubstantial with the March to the West, expresses:

> *Heaven and earth are everlasting*
> *but man must die.*
> *as old age is a wicked business*
> *charge, brave men*
> *and welcome death.*

Similar ideas, coined by a basic personality where equestrian and epic corroborate and condition each other, are common in the equestrian societies of the Third World: Bedouins, gauchos, and sertajenos are some of the best-known archetypes. Without going too far back, it is appropriate to recall the proclamation of Fausto Aguilar, one of the many brave countrymen who fought in our civil wars, when he ordered his braves to charge with a dry spear on a harsh winter dawn of the 19th century: "*take off your ponchos, boys, it's not cold in the other world*". Notwithstanding this manifest disdain for life in cultures where masculine courage is a central star around the planetary of the other patriarchal, fatalistic and violent values of the Uruguayan countryside of yesteryear, the idea of death and the uncertainty about what awaits us distresses "the miserable mortals" equally. They consider it either as an explicable failure of *natura naturata*, as a necessary contingency of the creature, or as a capricious design of the gods.

At the elitist end of the scale, that of the spiritual aristocracies of the West, European romanticism, self-qualified as a subculture of "*superior*" intonation, has a different idea from that of the South American cavaliers and, consequently, expresses its fear of death with other terms and other twists. The German poet Novalis described death as "*the serious sign of a great and distant power*". Death is no longer the gateway to the perpetual rejoicing of a carnal Islamic warrior fallen in combat against the infidel during the Holy War, the *jihad* of which so much has been said these days, but the "eternal night" (*die ewgenacht*) that draws in the distance a painful interrogation, a nagging doubt, and an anguished enigma. Such qualities, strictly speaking, are proper to the thoughtful contemplators of perishable humanity and not of death itself, indifferent to the declinations of philosophical nominalism and the pathos of literary currents.

SELF-DEATH OR COLLECTIVE IMAGINARY?

The "Self-death" constitutes a cultural feature of the individualization and personalization that Western societies have imposed on their members. The `asabijja` of the Bedouin of the desert defines as a body spirit that subsumes and erases the singular subject, as Albert Khaldun puts it with insightful clarity in the 13th century. But our civilization has privileged the solitudes of the human soul and individual rights. Life and death then constitute something personal, reserved to the consciousness isolated in the "I". Rilke, as an intellectual representative of the Austrian bourgeoisie, so often quoted by the Central European authors who, beginning with Max Scheler, have dealt with the theme of the metaphysical ultimacy of the living/dying creature, was concerned with the "self-death" and he did so with the tone common to all aristocracies that have much to lose by being robbed of the grace and beauty of their golden world. A poet, at last, his elegies recreated, from afar, the thoughts of Montaigne, that *gentilhommecampagnarde* of the French Renaissance.

Rilke was obsessed by the idea of death, of his death as a person, as a creator, as the bearer of sensations and feelings, of values and disvalues. In The Duino Elegies, in the Sonnets to Orpheus, in The Book of Hours, in The Notebooks of Malte Laurdis-Brigge, in the Song of Love and Death of the Cornet Christopher Rilke, the poet, wounded by life --

30

"c'esteffrayante, la vie" protested Cezanne, the painter-- engaged in a memorable fight with death, aided by the Angel and the Lord. These helpers were indispensable, of course, because it was a matter of nothing less than his own irresistible death:

At an earlier time and in a different language, but with an identical tone, Montaigne expressed, "all the time you live, you take that away from life: you live it at its expense. The continuous task of your existence is to erect the building of death. You are in death while you are in life, or in other words: you are dead after life; but during life, you are dying, and death attacks the dying more harshly than the dead, more vividly and more essentially".

Death itself, in short, constitutes a kind of Gothic stained-glass window that does not let us see outside, but rather decomposes and plays with the light and shadow that penetrate the cathedral of life, that personal building that every man builds with the materials of a spirit-body that has him standing on the world and relates him to it. But the entrance into life and the consummation of one's own death transcend the consciousness of the singular man. When he is born, he does not have the slightest notion of this event because the extra-uterine consciousness has not yet been constituted, although the subconscious sometimes keeps within itself the trauma of birth, that rude shock that crumbles us from the warm security of the maternal nest and remains forever internalized in us. No other thing is the sudden shudder that sucks us in when we are about to enter sleep and, in such a way, startles us and leaves us trembling.

Some explanations venture that this sensation of collapse is a reminiscence, written in the genetic message, that evokes the fear of the fall, and even the very fall of the tree that our hominid ancestor inhabited, before the stage of the biped australopithecine, the *proto-homo-viator* of the South

African steppes. However, perhaps it is the psychic evocation of the departure from the womb, welcoming and unifying, and the shocking entrance of the body into an inhospitable and fragmented world, into an aggressive external environment. This capital event, as painful as a tear, will not only overwhelm the newborn child but will also make it cry. This action, as a response to a moving surprise, to the dissociating presence of cold, to noise, to the helpless loneliness of one's own body, makes the child breathe the atmospheric air and fully brings it into life. There is no personal consciousness of birth, or at least it is supposed to be so. But when a man dies, he has no consciousness either, for he has already resigned that consciousness to the power that takes it away from him. The soul, if it exists, is no longer linked to the body, to the neuronal system, to the chemistry of the brain. It is not consciousness but wakefulness for what is to come, either as punishment, or as a reward, or as an endless pilgrimage.

In the interim, let us call life if we refer it to the pause that links the preliminary non-being with the final non-being, more than one will evade the prowl of death with Epicurus' rhetorical gambit: *"while I exist, death does not exist; when death exists, I no longer exist"*.

This phrase, which after all is a challenge to the *"dispersion of matter"*, responds to a general orientation of the spirit that some link with the ontological horizon of modern science, as taught by Carse. However, Max Scheler mentions it as *"metaphysical frivolity"*. The *"absent presence"*, as he calls death, first as an idea and then as a reality incarnated in a finitude that neither forgets nor forgives, will have to impose itself on nonsense and cynicism.

But the tendency of the human species towards death - the search for Eros results, in the end, in an encounter with Thanatos - pointed out by Freud in the psychic field, clashes with the findings of ecologists studying the input and output of the energy that recycles living matter and then subsumes itself in a cosmic dump of ambiguous sign. While the psychologist denounces a thanato-tropism consubstantial to the human spirit, the biologist, in association with the ecologist, recognizes that life and death inhabit adjacent territories separated by osmotic membranes, so to speak. Claude Bernardaffirmed that*"Life is death"* as he witnessed the relentless eating of one another in the successive links of the food chains. Just as the shadow follows the body, death follows life, not as an insurmountable pothole but as a *continuum* and, instead of denying it, corroborates its *"surprising, paradoxical and scandalous"* character, according to Morin's concept. Indeed, despite the inevitable individual landfall in death, life is a stubborn wisp that sails upstream on the river of entropy, the relentless destroyer of all things. This against the tide march has been called negentropy, dientropy or epicthesis, according to the different treatises, and its restorative tendency overflows the biotic field. Indeed, that progressive decline towards the maximum disorganization with which Carnot and Clausius threatened us in the 19th century, thus decreeing the "thermal death" of the Universe, has today been questioned by the new astronomy. On the reverse side of the black holes, devourers of space, time, matter, and energy, the quasars, the white springs, seem to open. The *yin and yang*, the dialectic of opposites, would thus confront us with a cyclic universe that refreshes the degraded energies and entrusts them with new tasks in the inventions and super-inventions of a reiterated and incessant *Fiat Lux*. And this would not only occur on a stellar scale, but also on a galactic or even megalactic scale.

But we must return to the home of men and the problem of one's own death that concerned Rilke and was the objective of Socratic philosophy: *"true philosophers make dying their profession"*. This self-death takes place in the domains of the

Ego, in the singular corporeality and psyche of each terrestrial human being, regardless of his personal belief in the absolute annihilation of the mind, superstructure of flesh, and bone, or in the effective, though unproven, immortality of the soul. Death itself separates, privileges, and personalizes. It also decrees the end of the existing relationship between slaves and masters, by equating them with the rupture of their mutual dependence and confronting them with their own individual end.

The idea of death, the expectation of death, and the struggle with death--that is, agony--constitute the curtain of shadows that grants meaning and limelight to each person on the social stage and in private intimacy, bearer of talents and virtues, of pities and frustrations. And, at the same time, adding up the innumerable singular deaths that in the human world have been, it builds the great wall of the ecumenical necropolis on which the *tejné* and *poiesis* of societies and historical cultures are cut out. Each social class, which is also a type of civilization, exhibits a different conception and perception of death, linked, in turn, to a different conception of life. One dies as a man but also as rich or poor, as happy or unhappy, as oppressor or oppressed, as a personal fragment of a specific societal stratification, death makes us all equal but cannot, by retroactive effect, invade life and modify the relations of production and the injustices and inequities created by men in their millenary struggle for power. Death emerges, after all, as a *kratophany*, as a superior display of timeless majesty superimposed on the temporality of the lords of the world, masters of lives and estates but not of their absolute durability. A medieval dance of death anthologized by Menéndez y Pelayo, in his crude and clumsy way of speaking, corroborates this:

> *(Death says)*
> *Strong king, tyrant, who always stole*
> *All your kkingdom and filled the ark,*
> *Of making justice very little you curred,*

As it is notoriouos by your land.
Cometh to me, for I am monarc,
That I'll seize you and another higher one,
Arrive at the courtly dance in one leap,
In pursuit of you the Patriarch will follow.

MEMENTO MORI

Remember that you are going to die.

That is the warning of the *memento mori* that buzzes around us with the pertinence of a millenary bee. The only animal that meditates on death, that has the experience of the death of the Thou and the Other, and that awaits -- *"uncertain death, uncertain hour"*-- the definitive instant of its bodily annihilation (the turn of the worm, the retinue of putrefaction, the physical return to the mineral elements) is the man. That is why he calls himself mortal, making a noun from the adjective.

In our semantics of conscious finitude, mortal is thus equivalent to man, insofar as death appears, perhaps, as the tapestry where the tapestry of life is woven and the scissors of Atropos that cuts the thread of existence. The notions and preconceptions of vulgar thought are corroborated at a physiological level by an organized resistance that eventually gives way: Bichat considered individual life *"as the set of functions that resist death"*. As life is judged, so will death. There will be those who will flee from it as from a punishment. It follows as we have already seen - both on the ontic and psychic planes - that each one must elaborate the cocoon of his own death so that life may have "love, meaning and urgency".

But the fact of belonging to a subculture with a particular conception of the afterlife and mortality imposes on the person the coercive categories of the collective imaginary.

Consequently, one's own death declines as decreed by the social eschatology determined by the warrior or pacifist, chivalrous or villainous, contemplative or active, miserable or self-complacent, proud or pious accents, which constellate the values of the community to which the subject belongs.

On the obverse side of the biotic hominid, which after all is a bundle of instincts clinging to the dictates of conservation and reproduction of the species, stands the cultural hominid, a creature that knows it is going to die. This creature sought, beginning with the neanderthal funerary objects, and perhaps even much earlier, to placate the dead as the executor of a death not yet nominalized or symbolized. Much later, when elaborating the logical and analogical abstractions of civilization, man turned Death into the corollary of a reiterated vicissitude of singular deaths. Thus mortal beings, *"dreams of a shadow"*, as Pindar and Sophocles put it, and children of civilizations that are also mortal, as Valery poetized, mint the coin with which one can buy the good things of life and that one day they will deposit in the lap of death. This, and nothing else, means the obol for Charon's boat.

The "afterlife", reward or expiation, absolute finiteness, or perdurability of a soul forever freed from the dirty burden of matter, is not a free gift: it is acquired or alienated according to the omission or the fulfillment of actions and attitudes approved by the morals in use. This is well known to religions whose dogmas and liturgies act as synallagmatic contracts between men and the sacred.

"The bow's name is life, though its work is death", said Heraclitus the Obscure, although not so much for those who have deciphered his cryptic language. This was also understood or intuited by those who preceded or succeeded the Ionian thinker. We men act according to implicit or expressed historical projects that we transmit to our children and grandchildren. We act thinking that although life will pass away, our personal deeds and acts remain; *"live life in such a way that it may stay alive in death"*. With this point of view, the attainment of fame is a vicarious way of surviving, and therefore the greatness of the *"causes"* is entrusted to the memorable survival of its supporters.

The fatherland, the religion, and the party have walked through history on a litter of dead people who fell convinced of the survival of their name and their spirit, if not of their immolated body *pro aris et focis*.

We have thus reached the extreme level of discourse, the limit, and its necessary extinction. If we do not frame the *memento mori* that we all carry on our backs as fleeting snails of life, we run the risk of losing ourselves in the nebula of abstract answers instead of asking specific questions.

There is general agreement on the theme of the physiological erosion imposed by the time we live: every hour hurts and the last one kills. But the question that ends up being metaphysical and/or theological is that of death itself, while the ultimate ethical question concerns personal death within the culture that has elaborated an ideology of death and in whose name it demands the adoption of certain valuable behaviors and the condemnation of certain transgressive behaviors. Here we introduce, and certainly not by smuggling, the theme of Evil and all the satanism that have been in the world. However, as the brevity of the discourse obliges me to develop only the theory of death, I reserve the tenebrous subject of the devil for later meditation.

An ethnology of death must begin its work by comparing bodies of beliefs and customs about death in a diachronic and synchronic sense. Day by day the number of scientific studies dedicated to punctual essays and large synoptic panoramas on the topic is growing. As our unscrupulous culture of waste buries its head in the ground, like the ostrich -- who can forget this exercise in prestidigitation denounced in Aldous Huxley's American novel: **After Many a Summer Dies the Swam** -- the efforts of academics to question social groups about their respective visions and exercises of life, intimately related to the conceptions and funerals that ritualize the paraphernalia of death, are redoubled. To this ethnology of human finitude, we must turn then to understand, as Morin expressed, why our societies and cultures *"do not function only in spite of death, but by it, with it and in the mind"*.

THE DESPENADORA AND THE I.C.U.

The ceremonies of passage that mark the stages of human life -- birth, baptism, initiation into adulthood, marriage, family celebrations -- are replicated in the rituals of death. The agony, the wake and the final destiny of the body -- burial in the Earth, exposure to the Air, consumption by Fire or immersion in Water, that is, the return to each of the Four Elements of the primordial *arkhé* that, according to Empedocles, constituted the "roots of all things" -- give rise to a series of practices that vary from culture to culture and from time to time. Behind this pious horizon that sacralizes the spaces of the here and now, the symbolic fan of the conceptions of the Afterlife unfolds. In this way, the different doctrines concerning the new activities of the souls of the deceased are historically articulated according to the respective dogmas about the survival of that breath that gave strength, grace, and expressiveness to the perishable flesh. And, as a corollary, beliefs are generated concerning the system of retributions that the superhuman entities grant to the immaterial portion of those who, during their residence in the matter, were virtuous or sinners.

In the decision-making centers of contemporary Western civilization, there is a deliberate effort to conceal the existence and persistence of death in the world, understanding as such not the planetary globe but the plexus of realities that constitute social everyday life and give meaning to the object prostheses that result from the transactions of the Lebenswelt with the environment.

A sign, perhaps a minor one, emerges from commercial propaganda: undertaking is no longer undertaking, since they have become "provident". Another sign, this one of capital importance, can be seen in the treatment given to the topic of death by the sportsmanship and youthfulness of a culture whose behaviors and attitudes, endorsed by the postmodernist axiology in vogue, seek to minimize the inevitability of death, whose tragic shadow loomed over the feelings and thoughts of previous generations.

Barrán has exemplarily raised the problem by studying the successive and antithetical accents of death and dying in the "barbarian" Uruguay, which was suddenly rich, spontaneous, and vitally authentic, and therefore memorial of death and its carrion, and in the prude Uruguay of concealment and falsification of the funerary. This last period, whose critical culmination we are witnessing, started, if we accept the date proposed by the aforementioned author, around 1860, the time of *"disciplining"* --or of a new escape to *Laputa*, according to Swift's intentional term?-- turned out to be the country whose exquisite corpse we are watching over today without having yet become aware of the great national ethical obituary that has some of us terrified, many more bewildered, and all of us cursing.

Nevertheless, today there are peasant and pre-literate cultures that feel the impenitent presence of death and include the society of the dead in the society of the living. They thus preserve in their practices and beliefs the primitive Greek meaning of the word cemetery, **koimeterion**, that is, dormitory or collective bedding place, if translated literally.

THE COMMUNITY OF THE LIVING AND THE DEAD

There is a tacit community between the living and the dead whose memory we have lost, except for the increasingly declining floristry of November 2, the official jubilee of the dead. Mexico aside, there is perhaps no other nation today where coexistence with death is viscerally incorporated into popular culture as in the case of rural China. I could feel the pathetic validity of such fraternity in both countries but now I want to refer, apart from the memorable Mexican calacas, to the dialogue that in certain parts of China life and death maintain.

When I was traveling, years ago, through the troglodytic villages of Shenshi, in the agrarian heart of that giant of a thousand faces that is the Asian country, I came across a reiterated colloquy that manifested itself directly, without any kind of gaps, neither epistemological nor metaphysical, to those who knew how to walk with their eyes wide open through the ancient fields.

The dwellings of the farmers, and not houses - the house is the womb of family life and for that reason, it is called a dwelling -, were not built on the agricultural land nor were they founded on the sterile soil. They were caves excavated by the work of a millenary craft of human moles. They plunged into the cliffs, twisting their tortuous corridors in the orange sandstone of the walls.

But above their subterranean intricacies, up there, in the air and in the light, were the wheat fields of the cereal areas sown since the early Neolithic. To clarify things for those who have false stereotypes about Chinese agriculture, in this part of the country wheat is the food grain par excellence; rice, on the other hand, is the typical cereal of the flooded eastern and southern monsoon territories.

The wheat fields stretched out on the plains of yellowish earth, sometimes wounded by the scars of the erosion that undermines the soil of the whole area. The horizontal monotony of the fields, however, was broken by the half-ruined mounds of the tombs. In those hundreds, thousands of tombs, slept the remains of grandparents and countless farmers who had built those landscapes and left in them the fertilizer of their love and their bones, their work and their excrement -- human excrement, in Chinese, is called, demurely and poetically, **"night soil"** -- according to a cyclical swing between the yin of life and the yang of death.

The tombs barely shown above the army of spikes that tightly surrounded them, as if trying to get into them. Likewise, the bones of the ancestors, testimonies of the architecture of a life that was not resigned to die completely, were leaning out to the wind and the fullness of the day, overflowing the ruinous stone undercuts. An invisible geology of lime, sprouting from the tombs, fertilized the bread-bearing lands and poured its minerals into the scarce water of the streams. The living beings slept, loved, reproduced, and died in the darkness of the chambers dug in the rock. They, in a way, turned out to be the dead and buried, while the dead up there, those who extended above the cavemen, became the true living.

Insensitive to the punishment of the meteors - the burning of the sun, the dryness of the air, and the fury of the storms - the dead watched over the ferocity of the fields and guaranteed the good faith of the harvests. With the song of the birds and the elytra of the insects, mimics of their ancient extinct voices, they sacralized the work of the children who went in search of water, of the peasants who were already preparing the harvest, and of the little women dressed in black who glided, erect as caryatids, carrying bundles on their heads and who were suddenly lost among the ripe ears of corn.

When I remember those now distant hours, gratified by the ceremonious smiles of the simple and wise people of Shenshi, I think that we, men of the cities, have brutally cut the ties that united us with the womb of the Earth, which is not only the womb of what lives and flourishes but also the resonant box of the cosmic rhythms, every day more distant from our chronometers and our business conception of time. To free ourselves from a clumsy innocence--the *"rural idiotism"* according to Marx, the *"blind countryside"* according to Léfèbvre--as we say in proclaiming our enlightened rationality, we have mounted this charade of existing and consisting-- which are not properly of the Being--which, in order to flee from the Non-Being, devitalizes and alienates us.

The popular religion of the origins did not separate the spirits of things - **orenda, manitou, mana**, **and He** - from the very things moved or suddenly inhabited by them. The tributary cultures of Judaism, Christianity, and Islam separated the Creator from his Creation, the Maker from his Creatures, the **Natura naturans** from the **Natura naturata**. In such a way a moat was dug between the divinity and men and the collective informal way of addressing with the **mysteriumfascinans** disappeared. Instead, the formalities of the liturgy were appealed to, which, with the passing of the centuries, became more and more mechanical. In order to elude it - there were always

44

people with their backs turned to the divine - the denial of any deity or theodicy, of any psychopomp entity, of any kind of soul or spiritual survival was reached. And so it was that in the end, the representatives of the so-called Faustian style of civilization, in opposition to the Arcadian style of agrarian man or the magical forestry man, put life on one side of the scale and death on the other. We thus forget that both, life and death, constitute the complementary phases of the same reality which peasants traditionally recognize and ecologists scientifically legalize. Indeed, the chemical work of the microbiota returns the constituent matter of the organisms to the terrestrial matter (that is, earth and water at the same time) while an input of energies, alone and through chlorophyll function, recycle it and open the way to the miracle of the renewal of life.

To further darken the spiritual panorama of our time, the recourse to personal union with God, the supreme expedient of the mystics, has also been called for. Except in the anachronistic islet of the Sufis, no one trembles anymore like the Quakers of yesteryear, nor faces the Absolute like the Swedenborgians. Nor is the belated trembling of the charismatics sufficient to engage hand in hand with the sacred, source of the Love that devours and the Light that blinds. We have nothing left but ourselves. This is the height of poverty and perdition. That is to say, the final triumph and the definitive pomp of death.

AFRICAN PYGMIES AND DEATH

All the Golden Ages, from that of the Yellow Emperor to that of Oblivion, show a humanity at the margin of death or, at least, favored by a sweet and insensitive death. In the mythical universe of the Central African pygmies, death also did not exist in the beginning. The anthropologist Paul Schebesta, who lived among the Bambuti and wrote a detailed study about them, tells us the following myth which, with little variation, I transcribe below.

Before the Origins there was nothing but God. God then made three children: two were male and one was female. One of the males was the ancestor of the pygmies and the other the ancestor of the blacks. God had contact with his creatures but never appeared before their eyes. Moreover, he had threatened his children with an evil spell if they sought to see him.

The woman was in charge of placing at the entrance of God's hut the wood for the fire and the container for the water. One hot afternoon, when she was bringing him the water, she succumbed to the curiosity that was bubbling inside her and decided to spy on her father, always hidden in the shadows of the shelter. No one would know but her, she thought to justify herself. And so, she hid behind the doorpost, waiting to see even a glimpse of the divine creator. God, at last, stretched out his arm, all adorned with rings of shining brass, to pick up the vessel. Happiness at last! She had beheld God's arm sumptuously adorned. Her heart leaped in her breast, rejoiced and grateful.

But God, who sees all things, knew at once of the woman's sinful curiosity. And after the fault came the punishment. He got angry, called his three sons, and condemned them jointly responsible for the sin of the peeping female. Then he announced to them that he would retire. From then on, they would have to live and manage without him. He boarded a canoe and took off down the river. No one saw him from then on.

The water, the animals, the roots, and the fruits, which were given spontaneously, also went with God. To get food, men would have to work, to sweat, to suffer. Moreover, something terrible would happen to them. And so it was. The withdrawal of God left among men the fatigue of work and the fatality of death.

The myth, pure or contaminated, reiterates the quality of scapegoat that the woman has had, it is imprudent Pandora, of all times on the Epimetheans, those who think after the fact, they unload the responsibility of their errors and deviations. But what is of interest here is the introduction of death in humankind and the dramatic circumstance that it fell to the marvelous human female, the bearer and giver of life, to fulfill a mission that in the end conferred upon her the ambivalence of a two-faced and therefore ambiguous symbol.

BETWEEN EUTHANASIA AND MURDER

The archaic man, like the archaizing man, is not afraid of death but of the dead, or even better, of the transit from life to death, of the contaminating combat of agony. Consequently, the dying person must die quickly and definitively so that in the last struggle, when the hesitant soul leaves and enters again and again in the body, it does not spread the nefarious "double" that would harm the members of the house and of the neighborhood, making them all sick without remedy.

In our Creole societies, tributaries of the indigenous, the Iberian European and the African, the traditional cultures have preserved, in some inland places, a character with thanatophoric characters, whose presence lasted until the first decades of this century and perhaps still survives, although stealthily, to avoid police complications.

It is the figure of the despenadora -- Death is a woman, not a man -- whose fearful and at the same time necessary activity survives in the minds of the old inhabitants of the Uruguayan countryside. In our Sanducer family, for example, there was talk of the despenadora of Buricayupí, the homeland where my father was born around 1891.

I heard the story about the arts of that despenadora when I was a child from the lips of my great uncles, the knife-makers Siceo and Adrián Marote, men with hair on their chests who only show fear at the glare of the luces malas [Popular myth in Argentina and Uruguay consisting in a light that appears at night and scares people looking at it] the and the wailing of the souls in pain. And I repeat it just as I heard it in the manor house on Misiones Street, in my native city of Paysandú.

The Buricayupí'sdespenadora was summoned by the relatives when the agony of the mourner became unbearable for him and his family. They not only suffered from the anguish of the dying but also feared the harmful effects of the lethal aura emanating from the struggle. When the craftswoman of death arrived, brought between dawn and midnight, she would come all covered and silent, conscious of the seriousness of her task. Without saying a word, she would go to the room of the dying man and would ask out to those who surrounded him. Once alone, she would take off her shawl, roll up her sleeves and then make the sign of the cross. She would lay the patient face down and gently and deftly place her right knee on his lumbar vertebrae while, at mid-height, she held his chin with one hand and his legs with the other. She would briefly weigh the body, calculated the expenditure of energy, and waited for the right moment to practice the maneuver. It seemed as if she was going to stay still forever, like the unfurled wings of a dark butterfly, when suddenly, with a quick movement, she sank her knee and raised her arms in unison, breaking the backbone of the dying man.

The crunching sound could be heard even on the other side of the house, one of those bearded men of good memory told me, trembling as he evoked it: such was the universal silence that reigned while waiting for the outcome of the operation. Death then came suddenly and cleanly, for the good of all. And after it, the despenadora, after crossing herself again, left as stealthily as she had arrived and was lost in the shadows, now torn by the cries of those who were beginning to mourn.

Armando Vivante, who narrates similar cases that occurred in the Argentine countryside, offers other similar American examples, although some are charged with an accent of ferocity that distances them from the neat efficacy of the despenadora.

The Indians of Puno, Peru, hanged the dying man so that he would not throw out the abscess and make those present sick; the Huicholes of Mexico rubbed the dying man until he perished as a result of the merciless mashing; the Guaycurúes of the Chaco called the sorcerer of the tribe, who squeezed the stomach of the terminally ill man to the utmost and only released him from this terrible pressure when he felt him flaccid, collapsed, absolutely dead.

These examples of death by force are not homicides but ritual maneuvers, as in the pre-Columbian era was the Nahua death by an obsidian blade. Those who condemn such practices in the name of the charitable values of Western culture were yesterday sacramentalizing the atrocities of the Flanders and the genocides of the conquerors of America, while today, they justify the bombings of the Iraqis in Israel or the massacres provoked by American missiles in Baghdad.

The apparent cruelty of pre-literate and peasant cultures in the above-mentioned cases--there are others of infanticide and gerontocide based on reasons of group survival in the face of famine or environmental calamities--reveals that death is a matter that concerns everyone and not the personal self alone. The dying person from cultural areas foreign to our Judeo-Christian cosmovision of life knows, from the inside, the thanato-philosophy of his group and knows that death is a social and not a private business. Only in this way is it possible for him to accept with resignation, and even with a conviction, the rigor of the supreme ceremony of passage.

THE LANDSCAPES OF THE AFTERLIFE

But what lies beyond death? Does the death of the body also entail the annihilation of the vital breath that animates it? Is there a soul, a double? Is there a realm, a sacred space in the shadow of worldly or mundane space, where the souls of the dead will reside, whether rewarded for their good deeds or punished for their bad ones?

Will humans be judged twice, once at the death of the person and again at the Last Judgment, that chilling moment when the bodies of all, those of the dead in the tombs and those of the living in the full exercise of their lives, will compassionate at the sound of the trumpets to be weighed, measured, saved or condemned until the consummation of the centuries?

In short, what awaits the dead: total extinction or the survival of the divine flame that animated their mind and flesh during their residence on Earth?

These questions put us in the eye of the storm. In the eye of the storm, contrary to popular belief, there is a real calm and not a terrifying whirlwind. The eye of the storm when talking about death is the dialectical sphere that opposes meditation to turbulence, the calm of thought to the nightmares of terror. In this backwater of the theological storm, while the surrounding hurricane carries away the litter of the bodies and the souls fly like crazy fireflies, the millenary ideas about

immortality, transmigration, and reincarnation of those are installed.

In addition to the unquestionable destiny of singular
souls, there is the terrifying totalitarian mediate nature, which
excludes no one, represented by the Last Judgment, the Apoc-
alypses, and the Chiliasms, present in Christianity and other
religions.

These, and not others, are the transcendent matters that
fertilize the field of the sacred, which alludes to a separate reality, *sacer*, where the belief systems related to the Afterlife
make sense.

Such systems are multiple, as are the concepts of religion. In fact, this universal of culture[6] means, from its possible
etymologies derived from Latin, different and at the same time
concomitant things. There are at least four possibilities that explain the literal meaning of the word religion; Cicero's
relegere supposes the rereading, the strict observance of the
ritual that the Romans, jurists, and people who take everything
literally from all codes, divine, and human, fulfilled at the al-
tars of the gods; the *relinquere* of Macrobio points to the re-
spectful and even fearful distance that must be kept from objects and symbols of a sacred character; the *reeligere* of St.
Augustine means to choose again, to prefer definitively that
which, having been loved and believed in the beginning, was
abandoned to fall into sin; the *religare* of Lactantius alludes to
the powerful bonds of piety and faith that bind with God.

For atheists and agnostics, there is no immortal soul that
can escape the trap of death, and if there is, it is not possible
to prove its existence. For believers in the presence and

---

[6] The "Universals" of civilization have been thoroughly analized by
M. H. Herscovits, **Man and his Works. The Science of Cultural
Anthropology**. A. Knopf, New York, 1948.

persistence of the soul, the options are different, there are religions that exalt the perpetuity of life and religions that have perfected the validity of death as absolute dissolution and stillness of the soul. The explanation of this contrast introduces us to the meaning of life, death, and immortality in Christianity and Buddhism, to cite no other examples.

Both religions, the one with God, and the other, the Hinayana variant, that of the Small Vehicle, without God, free its adherents from the uncertainties of an absolute ending or of an infinite following. Christianity, says Paul Landsberg, by introducing the survival of souls in relation to the ontological category of eternity, institutes a liberation from time, change, and earthly becoming, which condition the idea of death. Buddha's Buddhism, different from that of those who deified him, fought from its beginnings against samsara, the popular belief about the incessant and terrifying transmigration of souls, and in the end imposed, with the fullness of Nirvana - different from the Hinduism of the union of the individual soul, Atman, with the Absolute, Brahaman - the notion of rest, of the end, of annihilation of all thought and desire. Buddha's Nirvana is Nothingness and means to expire. Nirodha, its synonym, is equivalent to extermination, and the common root of both refers to the glacial stillness of the high mountains, where the cold freezes the organic matter and the humidity of space. The basic postulate of Nirvana agrees with the idea that before the perpetual flow and rebirth of the souls, sometimes in unclean animals according to Karma (retributive principle attentive to the punishment of the bad actions and the reward of the good ones), the establishment of death as a liberating term arises. Thus ends the dreadful question: in what form will I be reborn when I die? It is not immortality but death that Buddha assures his followers. "Christ promises a birth to which no death can befall. Buddha promises a death to which no further birth and therefore no further death can befall." I do not know if

Landsberg ever traveled to Asia to see the various manifestations of Buddhism there at close quarters like I saw and expe-
rienced them. The aspect he alludes to does not take into account the positive aspects of the salvation of Nirvana, as it
arises from the Buddhist doctrine itself and from the vision of
its adepts, serene thinking reeds, convinced of the beatific eternity they will enjoy after death. But what Landsberg points
out, while inevitably Eurocentric, can be accepted in general
terms.

We cannot and should not evade the symbolic circle of
our culture, or else, we will be left levitating in an emptiness.
It is impossible for a Westerner, resident in Europe or America, to assume "*orientality*" by reading a library or learning
Zen Buddhism in thirty lessons. To attempt to do so, as so
many do, is to commit cultural nonsense of the first magnitude.

THE THANATOCRACY OF THE I.C.U.

The archaic cultures of the past and the archaizing cultures of the present have promoted the extirpation of agony, the acceleration of death. The scientific-technical culture of our times proposes the opposite: to arm wrestling with death, to prolong life at any price, to oppose its almost infinite resources to the physiological claudication of the terminally ill patient.

Between these two extremes lies the European Christian civilization of the private ceremonial of death, when people died at home and in bed, while the family received the last wishes of the dying person, the sole and supreme officiant of the preparatory process of his funeral. The sick person, aware of his imminent death -according to what the family doctor announced or what he guessed from his inner certainty and the undisguised affliction of his relatives- handled, well or badly, with serenity or with scandal, his farewell from this world. On some occasions, it was the *nuncius* mortis who gave the news, but this formalism did not reach the generality of the dying and constituted a privilege of the ostentation that the dominant classes granted, for reasons of status, to the ceremonies of passage.

Aware of his approaching end, the seriously ill person then managed his last moments. He decided, if he had not done so before, the destiny of his goods, summoned his close and distant relatives, gave advice to his children and said goodbye to his friends, and asked forgiveness for the mistakes he had made during his life. Then, at his request, or that of his relatives, the priest would administer last rites. And everything happened in the domestic sphere, in the midst of a reverential silence disturbed only by the sobs of the women and whispers of the extended family that awaited the inevitable outcome.

When death came, the fading person, if he was not immersed in a feeling of deep sorrow, would expire conscious of the love and pain of his loved ones, and that affective certainty granted him peace, comfort, and courage to face the mystery of the Afterlife.

Around two decades ago, or even less, the cultural situations - which include the scientific ones, although many and mistakenly do not understand it that way - have changed.

The surgical, cybernetic, and pain medicine revolution, complemented by the techno-revolution of devices, have depersonalized the doctor-patient relationship. Of course, this happened in the half-ethical, half-social circumstance of the disappearance of the family doctor, who was both a scientist and a friend who encouraged and inspired confidence. This general practitioner no longer exists, and the mutual insurance companies have become the managers of anonymity, the dispensers of indifference and rudeness, if not of error.

This being so, every sick person who gets worse is transferred from home to the hospital or sanatorium, where death ceases to be a natural process and becomes a kind of disease, a challenge to the "great medicine". The greater the quantity and quality of science - a fact that is true in the seats of wealth and power but not in our shameful Third World environment - and the greater the speed and effectiveness of technology - here we only receive the technological junk discarded by the industrialized countries -, death becomes a problem to be solved. To try to solve it when the patient is young or curable is perfectly fine, but when the patient is besieged by expiration and the nature of the ailment does not allow any hope of recovery, the problem then becomes a perverse gibberish.

This irrationality makes its way, settles in, and finally becomes the norm because a leading sector of the new medicine has set out to demonstrate that death can be conquered, or at least postponed almost indefinitely. Thus conceived the general state of things, the civilization of the ICU replaces the sorcerer's charm or miracle-workers doing. And it goes without saying that it is the antithesis of the "civilized" version of death, understood as the ritual and merciful acceleration of death or euthanasia.

The ICU is a kind of Leviathan, an imperious and rapturous beast. No one can tear from its claws - polished and aseptic - anyone who has fallen into its clutches. The patient, isolated, visited briefly and impersonally by a medical team, assisted by skilled nurses who attend the patient to the beat of the stopwatch, immersed in a frosted and disinfected universe, is subjected to an impressive battery of serums, injections, artificial pumps, electrical stimulants, and external plastic and metal organs that replace his poor, claudicating entrails. He is surrounded not by the faint familiar voices of yesteryear but by the endless purring of electronic screens stitched by clots of light or shuddered by blue lightning. At times, in the intervals of calm, when the work of the machines and the swaying of the staff subside, a murmur comes from some secluded corner of the room, invaded by the violent odors of the pharmacopoeia, which flickers on and off like the flapping of wings, but nothing flies there, neither the flies, *"the familiar, inevitable gourmands"* of Antonio Machado, nor the angels of the legends.

When the patient can no longer speak, nor wink, nor even grimace; when he lies on his bed like a naked and defenseless mass; when he is besieged and conquered by the most absolute solitude, then, in that supreme moment, no one cares for the progress of his soul, for the course of his thoughts and feelings that still linger in his darkened mind. Accurate and soaked gadgets surround him as a cloth surrounds the insect fallen in them. His organic functions are managed from the outside and his decayed viscera, now useless, are replaced by a paraphernalia of remote sensors, thermometers, drop counters, laser beams, and feedback micro-machines that are in charge of keeping alive, if the term does not sound like an indecent mockery, the poor being imprisoned in that satanic workshop (I finally dared to use the adjective that had been haunting me from the beginning).

This fading person of the industrial civilization has not been able to handle his death trance, neither morally nor affectionally: it has been handled by the scientific-technical system as a metalogical issue rather than a pathological one, and it goes without saying that the theological has been out of all possible consideration.

And when he finally dies wounded by stubborn needles, masked with carbo-chemical masks, subjected to the maneuvers (or tortures?) of a thanatocracy that only values the efficiency of its delaying, and not therapeutic, ingenuities, he has become a jumble of besieged flesh and captive limbs, a brainless and degraded waste, a dehumanized and desacralized shred. He dies ungrateful and alone; he dies in the fog of anesthetics and gases, with his conscience annulled; he dies without being able to purify his spirit, without being able to talk to himself, deprived of the will to face, with serenity or with dread, the trance of his own death.

This macabre painting, the passive obverse of the dance of death but no less terrifying than it, should not be considered as the literary product of my personal misoneism.

I am not an enemy of science or technology, and I believe in their earthly achievements of the human race. But those of us who have been very close to death, bathed in its warm and silvery waters, enveloped in its splendor and immersed in its music, rebel against its size. Perhaps someday I will tell -- I do not have much time left -- what I felt on the morning I began to die in a sanatorium in Bogota, when I was snatched, despite the muffled protest of my organism and my subconscious, from the welcoming tunnel through which soul and body, forever embraced, were drifting towards a Great Light. This soft and at the same time radiant beacon, apparently lit at the exit of what seemed to be a subway river, magnetized my senses and claimed me, intoning - a visible and audible entity at the same time - a kind of lullaby, a lullaby to introduce me into the sapient dream of that sonorous luminary that promised me.

In the meantime, and to conclude, let us remember the not so paradoxical phrase that Octavio Paz, the novice, the one I like, wrote around 1950 in The Labyrinth of Solitude: *"Tell me how you die and I will tell you who you are"*.

THE MASQUERADE OF THE LIVING AND THE DEAD

I. THE CARNIVAL AND THE HUMAN CONDITION

Now that the scattered stridencies of an ancient community festival, now transformed into a programmed, "authorized" and remunerated spectacle, have ceased, it may be appropriate to make some historical and anthropological considerations on the origin, development, and destiny of the carnival as a ceremony of life that, paradoxically, also summons the very remote rituals of death.

This episode, annually held under different names from an antiquity that goes beyond the Greek dyonisiai and the Roman saturnalia, has summoned, century after century, the novel attention of those who act it, contemplate it, judge it, or study it. The theatrical irruption of the irrational and the anarchic, the brief validity of an upside-down world, the unleashing of transvestism, the scandal, the license, the violence, and noise, in addition to other less notorious features, is a kind of earthquake that disturbs and questions the prevailing order throughout the rest of the year in civil societies.

It is also a break in the flow of everyday life, a breach through which the old allegories of time and space, of fecundity and expiration, of the serious and the comic, which invariably intervene and intermingle in the mundane course of our human life, "short, dirty, wretched and cruel", to put it in the disenchanted words of Hobbes, penetrate in spurts.

THE CARNIVAL, STONE OF SCANDAL

The carnival is a party, a collective event that in the past was shared by rural communities and urban societies and that nowadays is limited to the militancy of specific groups, as it happens in Montevideo's carnival.

This circumstance, linked to the apogee of mass culture, citizen anonymity, and the empire of television, has reduced it to a series of sound images, suitable to be contemplated rather than a drama to be lived, as it was in the times of its youthful apotheosis. Let me clarify that drama, in the original Greek sense, meant action, performance. Carnival, theatrically considered, is, however, much closer to comedy and farce, when not confused with it, as Umberto Eco claims.

The carnival - a name that appeared at the end of the fifteenth century and became widespread only in the seventeenth century in Europe - is used, together with other*designatta*, as we shall see, to denote a conjunction, at times confusing, of elements that integrate, no matter the era, the spiritual constants of the human condition.

In fact, the representative nucleus of the carnival is not univocal but multifarious. It constitutes a sort of estuary of festivities, ceremonies, and celebrations that take place in the winter months of the northern hemisphere, which cover the period from Christmas to Lent.

Those who want to classify it by only one of its characteristics are condemned to partiality, if not inaccuracy. Carnival appears at first sight as a collective masquerade. But upon closer examination, it turns out to be much more than that.

From the point of view of the philosophy of the festivity, the carnival embraces a series of survivals of archaic rites of fertility and of ultra-tomb mixed with the personal and collective attempt to free the soul of cobwebs and the body of bad humor.

The latter reveals that carnival, as *katharsis and pharmacos*, is rooted in the very existential structure of the psychosomatic. It is also subject to the daily tyranny of *nomos*, that is, the realm of convention expressed through the rules of fashion, custom, morality, law, and religion, each with its respective rites and liturgies.

In such a way it constitutes a rebellious and revolutionary expression, although devoid of any secular political or economic theory, in which is manifested, through scandal and fantasy, noise and havoc, violence and malice, those instincts and those passions repressed by the coercive mandate of those who command the destinies of the community.

The carnival appears considered as a convergence of diverse cultural currents in a significant plexus, as a polysemic creature, as a party, as a social game, as a theatrical farce, as a therapy, as a kind of unbridled madness, as a critique of the customs of the ruling classes and as a collective magic at the service of public health.

Its complex mythical and ritual plot, where the cosmic and the anthropic are indissolubly intertwined, places it on the margins of the pagan and the Christian, of good and evil, of the permitted and the forbidden.

It is at the same time each of the aforementioned things and something different that results, not from the sum but from the reciprocal empowerment of the same. In short, the carnival is nourished by a system of actions and passions, by a *paidia*, a*infatuation* and a saving activity at the same time, which are combined in two planes: one, the spontaneous and popular, with a rural bias, and the other, regulated and official, with an urban style.

The masquerade, the feast, the water and flour battles, the wigwams, the bears, the horses, the heifers, and the lady-bugs, etc. are the representative part of the popular and primitive carnival. The parades of eighteenth-century Rome, the Venetian masked balls, the parades of floats in Nice, and the group competitions in Montevideo's Parque Rodó, for example, constitute the municipalized and regulated *facet* of the civic carnival.

Mónica Rector speaks in this sense about the Dionysian and Apollonian versions of carnival, although the terms, attractive enough, are not entirely correct. The basic elements of the attitude towards carnivals --crazy dances, music that often provokes states of possession and even trance--are of a Dionysian, menadic, corybantic and bacchic type, and these aspects are intimately linked to the orgiastic and telesthetic undertones of popular religions. The Apollonian, which does not fit into the systematic disorder of the carnival, is related to another type of infatuation, the prophetic, analyzed by E.R. Dodds in his famous book The Greek Books and the Irrational.

But what is the spirit of carnival?

Pío Baroja, the novelist, who in the 1920s considered carnival to be a thing of the past, wrote in his essay **The Roots of Carnival**: "Carnival was surely man's most suggestive profane festival. It had all the attractions: brutal joy, satire, mystery, eroticism, perfidy, debauchery, revenge, and then the prospect of repentance on Ash Wednesday. The essence of it is debauchery and scandal..."

Carnival must therefore be defined by means of a Manichean type of opposition. Just as there is a *yin* there must be a complementary *yang*: nature and the human condition point it out continuously. The rivers flow out of their course to return

64

to it; the men of the traditional European world --and its oil stain spilled in the colonies-- get drunk, gobble food and delicacies in the style of Pantagruel, copulate like beasts, joke like fools, threaten like perverse thugs, laugh foolishly, indulge in unbridled games and go collectively wild during carnival because then Lent will come with its long face and its deprivations to call them to account and impose punishments on them.

According to this back and forth from the carnal to the spiritual, and vice versa, there is a perpetual counterpoint between the repressive constriction that sickens and the debauchery that cures. **Eros**, the Love, will emerge from the dialectical battle between these two states.

In this way, the people of all times had a period of time during which social rules were broken and life acquired a tone of freedom, excess, and discomfort.

This was linked to the mystical and mythical, to the phantasmal and fearful of an afterlife that, while being the domain of death, promised the renewal of life. By acting in such a way, the accents of the sacred guided the excess of the profane and, at the same time, allowed the earthly values (and disvalues), carrying on their shoulders the pitiful frustrations, clumsiness and insanities of the human, to take possession for a few days of their ascetic and tabooed territory.

That license, that of getting out of the trap of work and reverential fears, that leap over the silence imposed by the rules of treatment, by the peaceful customs and, by the religious precepts; that relapse, as some interpret in the primitive animality of gluttony and sex, or, as others prefer, in the primitive equality of the Golden Age, has been explained by sociologists, anthropologists, psychologists, and, above all, by psychoanalysts.

I will try to systematize the inquisitions and responses of them. And I will also say some things that, although I conceive them as my own, come from very far back, from that heritage of thoughts that we men of the West handle as the precious inheritance of the wrongly called pre-Socratics, terminal products of a tradition whose roots are even deeper than the cultural humus of the Neolithic.

Carnival is equivalent to carnal; to the flesh of men and women given to the debauchery of a fleeting encounter between strangers so that they will always remain so; to the meat and wine of unbridled feasting. Carnival is a vertiginously practiced game, with an excess of gestures, with a profusion of bravado and verbal scorn. Carnival is madness, ridiculousness, humorous meetings, and farce.

Likewise, it is costumes and masks that impose their mystery and discomfort in the midst of a deafening noise of shouts and laughter, of rattles and bellows, of explosions and percussions. Carnival is a kind of hysterical joy, at odds with the fresh effusion of true joy, and a boisterous mingling of people, animals, and things. Carnival is a reversal of social, personal, and sexual roles. All this is encapsulated in a series of indicators that underpin and corroborate the sense of nonsense, to put it in a way similar to a Cervantine pun that would not displease C. K. Ogden and I. A. Richards.

These carnival activities and paraphernalia have traditionally manifested themselves in a set of maneuvers and behaviors, namely: the sprinkling of water (natural and sewage); the stoning with pebbles and the staining throwing of rotten fruits and eggs; the mangling of wimps, dogs, cats and men, especially the eternal hooded fools that decorate the peasant heraldry of stupidity; the cockfights (and beheading); the beatings with bladders to women so that they have many children; the parades of cows, horses and bears shaped by means of frames and wires; the crowds and theories of giants and big heads; the marches with torches, as in the Italian carnivals of the Renaissance, and the burnings of old things that at the end will give fire to the fabulous Valencian Fallas; the flatulent noises produced with *ad hoc* devices; the crunchy obsessive swaying of the swings; the explosion of rockets, firecrackers and serpent firecrackers; the drumming of membranophonic instruments and the decomposed clanging of metallic instruments of high sonority; the piñatas of the first Sunday of Lent; the concealment of the face and body with all kinds of ridiculous paintings, gadgets and garments, the use of which confers on the lout or the gentleman who thus conceals himself the privilege of making a loud inventory of the sins and faults of his neighbors; transvestism, particularly that which cloaks men in women's clothing; aphrodisiac dances, full of obscenities; real or fake fights between the inhabitants of nearby villages; sexual excesses protected by anonymity and atrocious meals washed down with alcoholic beverages; the use of flour and bran to be thrown in the faces of passersby; the assaults and visits of groups of boys to houses where girls gather and their songs and dances are rewarded with sweets and drinks; the formation of spontaneous groups that compose together licentious or sassy lyrics and then (dis)sing them denouncing the abuses, perversions and tricks of the local men; the burial of Carnival through the burning of a doll or the mock burial of a laughable character, preferably the village idiot; the establishment of princes of mockery and abbots of unreason through the appointment of a Carnival King and his court; the pompous celebration of the Thursdays of comadres and compadres [godmother and godfather of your child] that precede the three traditional days -- Sunday, Monday and Tuesday -- in which the cups of madness are drunk and the stakes of a great promiscuous and solemn farce are raised, cheerful, aggressive and jocund at the same time.

CARNIVAL OUTSIDE EUROPE

These features, enumerative and not exhaustive, of the peasant and village carnivals of the Old World vary from country to country and from county to county. But as such, the classical carnival system reaches its maximum degree of intensity in Italy, France, and the Iberian Peninsula.

There are certainly multiple carnival ceremonies in Germany, England, Slavic, and Nordic countries of Europe, and there is no lack of festivities with a similar spirit in some Asian and North African regions. However, our attention should be focused on the Mediterranean cradle of carnival and, above all, on the Iberian Peninsula, from where the conquerors and colonizers of America came with a millenary civilization on their shoulders.

European carnivals disembarked in the New World and here they were transformed, vanished, or remained entrenched in the remote mountain valleys, shining with all their primitive splendor.

There is, consequently, an ancient carnival with regional and ethnic characteristics that has gone through a process of transculturation due to the physical and psychic presence of American aborigines and of Afro-Americans that incorporated the carnival celebrations of the genocidal of aborigines and slave masters.

Thus the Afro-Uruguayans incorporated the candombe to the Montevideo carnivals of 1870 and from then on their patches and their choreographic grace gave brightness and beauty to a popular celebration that, unfortunately, has already ceased to be so, overwhelmed by commercialization and television *kitsch*.

I take this opportunity to say, by the way, that our carnival is not a party of African origin as many believe.

The black people slipped into it because they had no other choice; having their rites, their myths, and their gods dead, they first celebrated their public ceremonies on Epiphany, and then they settled in the carnival that came from Europe and was acriolated in Montevideo.

A detailed study of carnival in Latin America would have to establish the characteristics of carnivals in the areas of cosmopolitan cities -Mexico, Caracas, Santiago, Buenos Aires, etc.- and the particularities of carnival in the Antilles and the circum-Caribbean area, the Brazilian coast and Montevideo, as far as the impact of African cultures is concerned, and the features of carnival in Mesoamerica and Andean America as far as the transfer of the European to the indigenous ethnic groups is concerned.

But in order to carry out this succinct investigation with a certain methodology, it is necessary to previously analyze the different aspects or subsystems of carnival.

At the end of this task, we will then obtain a sort of spectral scheme that can serve as a navigation chart to trace the generic features of the carnival world in the cultural complexes of Latin America, and, locally, in those of the Uruguayan carnival, which is broader and perhaps deeper and more inciting than the Montevidean one, which should certainly be considered with greater ethnological depth by scholars.

There is a fact that we must highlight beforehand. The European functionality of the carnival as a winter festival is lost in America. In the tropical area, high temperatures prevail throughout the year, while in the area where the seasons are differentiated, as in our country, the carnival falls in the middle of summer.

That limits a series of features and accentuates others; the parties disappear although not the drunkenness; the collective frenzy of the dance is attenuated and the dominance of the game with water in the streets is accentuated -those afternoons of my distant Paysandú, soaked with buckets- and during the assaults [to go to someone's house with snacks and drinks without notice] to the houses, as it happened in the Uruguayan carnival of long ago.

The European carnival takes place during the time when snow covers the agrarian landscapes and people must remain in their homes. Inactivity ferments the spirits. The acedia provoked by the lost hours in the heat of the home, that after the supper is restored by the traditional gracefulness of the gatherings when the legends and the stories are passed on and so the cultural identity from the old generation to the new one, acts like an incubus. The waters of concussiveness rise and people feel the need to open the floodgates, cure themselves of infatuations and expel the ghosts from the basement of their souls.

Then, from Christmas itself until Ash Wednesday, on the threshold of Lent, irrational riots and cathartic debaucheries break out, which at the end of a few days of gluttony, lust, agitation, intrigue, violence, concealment of the true personality, and assumption of a fictitious one, purge the body and the spirit and expel the inner demons. These operations are immersed in an ambiguous atmosphere of unreality and crude realism at the same time, within which circulates, like lightning and thunder, a mishmash of lights and noises that could be called infernal if it were not, as in this case, a human storm to the fullest.

In the same way, the remains of old fertility rituals are incorporated into these feverish and extraordinary hours, linked, as it could not be otherwise, with the cult of the ancestors, those larvae protectors of the life that grows and rocks.

When the earth awakens from its winter sleep and the wombs of the females give birth to offspring, these rites and magical winter operations will make the harvests abundant, that the calving of cows, mares, sows and sheep will provide the community with milk and meat, that the advent of children will ensure the renewal of human stocks, necessary to fight against the demands of Lady Death and multiply the arms that will serve agriculture, mother of the people. By studying the old festivities of classical antiquity in-depth, which is not good to call pagan because paganism was the religion of the peasants in the strict sense, it will be possible to explain how those ritual mechanisms worked and it will then be possible to understand the meaning of many things involved, since the dawn of humanity, in the dark marsupia of the carnival. Pierrot, for example, has his face painted in white and wears a white costume because he reproduces and evokes, without the eighteenth-century masked man knowing it, the pallor of the dead and their tunics from beyond the grave. Likewise, Harlequin is the Devil, the seducer, the tempter, the one who mixes things up, the evil emissary of Hell.

CARNIVAL AND SHROVETIDE: ETYMOLOGY AND SEMANTICS

Before entering the prehistoric arena of a festival that is a summary and compendium of others, gathering spirits from the Afterlife and playful rituals from this life, we must stop to examine the words carnival and Shrovetide. Under the stone of the word hides the crab of meanings.

Indeed, the *dénotatum* and the *designatum* of the terms can teach us a lot about their linguistic history, about the coming and going of the threads that weave the oral tapestry of cultures. That is why it is not a waste of time to ask about the origin of the words carnival and Shrovetide and the relationships between them.

Let us begin with the carnival, which in the Middle Ages the Spanish called **Carnal** and the French called **Charnage**, as it results from the **Bataille de Karesme et de Charnage**, the dry model that gave Juan Ruiz, the Archpriest of Hita, the subject for the confrontation of **Don Carnal and Doña Cuaresma** narrated by the Castilian poet in the brilliant **Libro de Buen Amor**[Book of Good Love]. To this Archpriest, of whose life nothing is known, the sackcloth of carnivalesque genius suits him well. For Menéndez y Pelayo he was a "libertine and tabernarian clergyman" with an "inhonest and anti-canonical life", while Amador de los Ríos considered him "a severe moralist and exemplary clergyman". Whoever wants to get out of doubt should consult (and enjoy) without delay the aforementioned poetic and novelistic work, which leaves more than one of the literary monsters of our time in the dust.

Returning to the etymology of carnival, let us say that the original word seems to have been *carnelevare*, which in Italian means to remove the flesh. After the three classic days of carnival comes Ash Wednesday and with it begins the time of fasting and deprivation of all kinds that is Lent.

Others speak of the Latin voices *caro, carnis*and *vale*, that is, farewell to meat, which repeats the meaning of the previous voice. Finally, there are those who fabricate a linguistic centaur and mix *caro*, meat in Latin and *avale*, gullet in French, which is equivalent to gobble down the meat. Carnival would then be the same as *carnal*, although circumscribed to the excessive consumption of meat that derived from the abundance of it: during the winter the animals that did not fit in the narrow peasant stables were slaughtered.

The European carnival was a time of gorging, drinking, and licentious practices. As a result of this last trait, the sexual connotations that constitute the other half of the word *carnal* would be well received. **Don Carnal**, and its licentious praxis, confer airiness and taste to a popular fruit seasoned by an age more applied to the delights of the body than to the contrition of the souls. Official history tells a different story, but the Middle Ages were a time of human plenitude, of enjoyment of life, in spite of the Black Death and the threats - neither so many nor so feared - of the flames of Hell. And proof of this is that very few people took the Lenten season with them, according to the documented complaint of the clergymen.

Thus, and for the above reasons, the etymology in question, which is not very convincing from a linguistic point of view, is in keeping with the excessive spirit of carnival, gobbling animal flesh and human flesh, the one on the tables and the other on the beds of all kinds, or on the side of the roads, or in the hayloft of the stables, or in the gloomy corners of the kitchens.

There is another etymology of carnival. For a long time the defenders of its exclusive Roman origin - a survival and conjunction of the *Saturnalia, the Lupercalia,* and the famous *calendae in March* - were seduced by the *currusnavalis* that paraded in the feast in honourto Isis, a transplanted Egyptian divinity, on March 5. From *currusnavalis* it would have passed to *carnavalis* and then to carnival. Nowadays this explanation, which was very popular in the last century, has been discarded.

Carnestolendas [Shrovetide] has a different flavor and a different history. It originates from the 13th century and comes from the Latin phrase *dominica ante carnestollendas*, that is to say, the Sunday before removing the meats, which would happen from Ash Wednesday, the portico of Lent.

In Spain, the word s*antruejo* in Castilian and *introido* in Galician are also used, and it seems that they have to do with the Latin *introito*, in this case referring to the days that introduce the severe territory of Lent. But what we have seen is enough.

The theme of meat has remained floating in the troubled waters where the demands of human appetites and Christian continence intermingle: Carnival thus becomes the last cry of gluttony in the harsh European winter, before the climate imposes food deprivation and the peasants begin a kind of period of quasi-hibernation.

Lent - imposed by the multi-secular wisdom of the Church - will administer last rites with a religious mandate of the peasants, fleetingly interrupted by the feasts, liberties, joys and follies of the carnival, a mythical escape to the Land of Cucaña, that painted by Brueguelel Viejo, or, if you prefer, a nostalgic return to the Golden Age, the good times of the reign of Kronos and Saturn, as Hesiod and Ovid tell us, when there was neither hunger, nor work, nor sickness, and one died "as one sleeps".

II. THE SEVEN MASKS OF CARNIVAL

The carnival is a complex phenomenon of culture as a symbol, convention, and behavior. Its allusions are multiple because its deep motivations and expressive modalities are also diverse. This multifaceted monster comes from the very heart of man, from the nest of his dreams and the funeral of his hopes. That is why, as a mirror of desires and an inventory of human failings, it both laughs and cries, interrogates and accuses, judges and condemns.

The carnival seems cheerful but it is not. Behind its jovial gesture lies the seriousness of magic; in the undercut of each laugh it distills the fertilized juice of melancholy; the tense arc of its farce, rather than the comic, points to the ridiculousness of an old-world whose ambition is eternal youth.

Faust appealed to the devil to recover it; the carnival calls the army of the dead and the ogres' troupe to obtain the fecundity of plants and wombs, to renew life in ecosystems and balance in human societies. This is the revolution of the carnival, to the etymological base of the letter: to return to the starting point after a brief and unsettling earthquake in the calm routine of institutions and conventions.

That is why it is a conservative and regenerative event par excellence. It happens so that everything remains as it is, according to the designs of the anti-dialectic astuteness that tradition, stepmother of village cultures, and the huddles around the fire, has always deployed.

FOSSILIZATION OF FORM; DEATH OF SUBSTANCE

When the carnival was a noisy collective party, personal filth and lacerations were bathed in the water of social lustration. The open-air debauchery then worked as a violent *katharsis*, purging the souls and soothing the bodies. Today we have been left without that great cauldron where we periodically submerged and macerated the funereal destiny and the craving for the immortality of the human creature, much more a slave of the past than a promoter of the future.

The past that repeats its ceremonies and routines is the paradisiacal orchard of the gods. The future is the territory of the feared change: there reign the infernal spirits of estrangement and the heresies of the new.

Disenchanted rationality, conciliatory urbanity, peaceful coexistence in dissent, and other forms of social control replaced when the materials of modernity were forged, the old multitudinous therapies applied outside any doctrine by the exorcising wisdom of the people.

Now, after so much theory thrown into the dustbin and so much ideology that smells of rottenness, we have dovetailed the evasion of drugs with the nihilistic manifesto of *rock* and, when we demand some certainty, lost in the fog of absolute nominalism, we are offered the defense and illustration of postmodernism as a perpetual *revival* of history, as spectacle and not as providence.

Deprived of the periodic help of the carnival, the human unconscious becomes dull after so many stumbles and bruises, and resorts --when it can afford it-- to the quackery of psychoanalysis. And if it cannot, it inaugurates new public and private expressions of violence, explores the forbidden territories of sex, and turns universal permissiveness into a license, so the tyrannical creature of the I make incursions into the underbelly of concupiscence, under the cover of the loincloth of "authenticity". It is truly pitiful to have lost the classic carnival with all that it had of ostentatious procacity and sharp fullness. Now that it is gone, because now the popular carnival -the spontaneous, unbridled and folkloric one, the one of magic and mystery- is dead, at least in the civilization of the West, I dedicate to its memory, which after all is remembrance, these pages that will seem daring to some and far-fetched to others.

In them, I will review the seven symbolic masks superimposed on a face that no man has ever contemplated because it is the effigy of a demon or perhaps of a god.

FULL MASK, FACE MASK, AND EYE MASK

The carnival appears as a protean enigma: its being unfolds and eludes us when we want to grasp or define it. That is why we must renounce to a total characterization of its essence and dedicate ourselves, with neat humility, to remove the masks and masquerades that hide a millenary mystery,

Full mask, face mask, and eye mask are not the same thing although they belong to the repertoire of subterfuges that conceal the immediate human and conjure demonic mediation.

I clarify, for the sake of understanding, that I am not speaking of the Christian demon but of the *daimon* of the ancient Greeks, that is to say, a spirit guide, a fertilizer of souls.

The mask is a piece of satin or velvet, sometimes black and sometimes white, which became popular during the carnival balls in the Italian salons of the seventeenth century. Behind its abstract concealment, there is an elusive, chameleon-like personality, carrying a poetic or evil proposal. Whoever wears it conceals the true features of his face in more than one sense, a mirror of the soul. The mask goes well with ballroom dancing wrapped with the silk paper of good manners. These, undoubtedly, are the gift of the *polis*, from which come the finely educated *poli* and the politician, who is sometimes very badly educated but does not care because he has the power: the *politesse* and police, even if they do not go together, spring from a common source. That is why the word that springs from behind that anodyne facade of the mask is not upsetting or rude. It can, however, be sharp as a sword or winding as a snake. The mask, in such a way, constitutes the alibi of civilization, the courtly resource of anonymity.

The mask is a human face whose features are exaggerated or deformed: it conveys ugliness, refers to horror or stupidity, sculpts with anthropic features the distinctive rictus of each of the seven deadly sins. Whoever wears it mimics the personality represented by it: it is the silly child, the malicious drunkard, or the unpleasant pimp. Behind the sign of the mask, the concomitant meaning unfolds.

The mask that revives the grimace of the mocker will incite mockery; that of the hypochondriac, to the gloomy farce. The mask is made of painted *papier-mâché*. An artifact concocted by human ingenuity, it also represents the human, the too human. The zoomorphic and monstrous world does not belong to him.

In order to enter this world, there are the masks ritually constructed with the sacred materials of nature: wood, fiber, bark, fabric, bristle, horsehair, shell, bone, and many others, sometimes of implausible origin.

The mask, in fact, has other functions and a different tradition. Its name derives, according to some linguists, from the Arabic word *mashara*, which menasjester or clown; according to others it comes from *masca*, which in Germanic, or perhaps in Celtic, meant witch.

From the Paleolithic paintings of shamans with masks shaping deer heads -the one from the Trois-Frères cave, for instance- or the strange effigies of ancient Egypt -gods with the face of a bird or jackal- the masking refers to the protective totem of the human group, to the world of the dead, to the cohort of goblins, to the personified forces of nature or to strange beings with hieratic features, whose facial architecture suggests fabulous origins. The ritual function of the prehistoric mask is repeated in the so-called savage peoples of the modern age, placed on the margins, or under civilization, by the arrogant umbilicalism of travelers, conquerors, and anthropologists themselves: Engels, for example, entered the ethnocentric and, therefore, bourgeois trap of Morgan, the lawyer turned ethnologist.

The mask constituted a fundamental element in the Greek *dionysiai*: the *tragoi*, the billy-goat generates the Greek theater by giving life to the satirical genre, typical of the satyrs, and after that tragedy and comedy open the way, sustained by the human voice that assumes and at the same time tells, didactically, the unhappy or glorious destiny of the gods, the heroes and the simple mortals.

The theatrical mask made of plaster, leather, and other materials has a mouth in the shape of a speaker. This megaphone is used to increase the volume and resonance of the actor's voice. It serves, as it was said in Latin, *per sonare,* and from there derives the name of *personaje* [character in spanish].

The Greek theater had three types of masks for the satirical drama and for those of the tragedy, they reached up to forty-one, according to the ages, the sexes, and the roles.

The mask introduces in the carnival the protective animals of the prehistoric horde, the clan of the sorcerers, the divinities, and the ghosts. Behind them unfolds the magical summons to the spirits from the grave to the genies of fertility, to the festive elves and gnomes. And there is also room for the grotesque joke, for the aphrodisiac insinuation, for the appeal to reverie and grace. It represents devils and apparitions, giants and ogres, fantastic fauna, and the teratology of Avernus. It brings together a motley collection of life and the hereafter. It introduces the gossip of misunderstanding, of illusion, of fantasy, of imitation, of malicious denunciation, of licentious sloppiness, of *castigatridendo mores*. But it also takes hold of the spirit of the user: it turns him into a force of nature, a messenger of the numens, a beneficent power, or an infernal emissary.

That is why I chose the mask and not the face mask or the eye mask to exemplify the seven temperaments of the carnival, that multifaceted alter ego of the human condition that begins the farce as a clown and ends as a guest of stone in the witches' coven.

CARNIVAL AS COLLECTIVE MAGIC

Magic is the anteroom of science and supplemental of religion. Religion proclaims the smallness of man before the superhuman: it is a vertical relationship of reverence and supplication. The hierotechniques, or techniques of the sacred, account for these attitudes of humiliation, adoration, and respect.

Magic proposes a relationship of domination, a horizontal extension of human power. By means of special maneuvers, rain is made to fall, the splendor of the ears of corn is propitiated, the ailments of man and cattle are cured.

The magician, by casting spells - and casting spells is nothing other than doing- moves the forces of nature and overcomes human wills, kills the enemy, and grants health to his neighbor. This magic is present in the classic carnival, in the one of peasant and village roots. The French André Varagnac has shown that the magical operations present in the carnival festivities, celebrated in the rural areas of his country from Epiphany to the beginning of Lent, are characterized by four main events: the visit of the fertilizing army of the dead to this "underworld", the purification of the houses from the bad influence of the sorcerers, the imposition of peace between the couples and the families, and the obligatory engagement of the youth.

It shows, in addition, that the masks figure the ghosts and that as in France, in Austria, according to the studies of Otto Hofler, the carnival band integrated by young people evokes the irruption of the souls of the deceased whose return to the world renews life. These young fun-lovers visit the farms, dramatize grotesque scenes, perform water sprinkling and flour sprays that have a sympathetic character.

The water cleanses of all evil; the flour promises abundant bread and, by extension, food in all seasons. Unfaithful husbands are also denounced and effigies are burned. In a parallel and complementary way, marital concord is celebrated and the officiants are then the giants and big heads, who as envoys from the Afterlife, bind the couples to be prolific while they gobble food to full cheeks so that there is no shortage in the family pantry.

Hence the feasts at the foot of his shadow: the high belly of the peasants predicts good food for the whole community, now and forever. Saturn, Kronos, and Gargantua, the ogre-parents, officiated from the culture of the megaliths, stony houses of the dead, as munificent protectors of the community, as devourers and creators at the same time. That is why the carnival is also a clandestine braguetazo [to marry someone for money], a begetter of children under the cover of drunkenness and rotten pots and pans.

The magic of carnival is much richer than the one summarized in the previous example. The presence of horses and bulls in the costumed parades is a reminder of breeding and hunting. The bears, which at the end of winter sprout from the caves, symbolize the renewal of life. The punishments with bladders to women, medieval echoes of the Roman saturnalia, are also a magical operation to attract on them the goods of fertility.

CARNIVAL AS THEATER

Music, singing, dance, and ritual go together. And from this mimesis of masked, possessed, and enthusiastic people (that is to say, inspired by the gods) the theater will finally emerge, something to watch, a spectacle. The carnival involves a collective activity of singular theatrical *vis*: it is satirical, it is comic, it is dramatic.

Its characters dialogue and establish a counterpoint of souls: there is an *agon*, a struggle of emotions, passions, wills, and destinies. The primitive Dionysian dithyramb sought to awaken the fecundity of nature. Propitiated by the spirit of wine, the theater arose to unleash the fecundity of words and give life to the pathetic dialogue.

The feast becomes theater and the theater disciplines the effusion of the feast and the carnival. Nevertheless, it cannot detach itself from its roots: the *parresia* that frees the words, the predisposition to sex, the vertigo of the dance that is after all the exterminating vertigo of the *moiras*, stronger than men and gods. Beyond the comic and the satirical, the carnival is chorus, actor, and choreographer at the same time. But instead of being immobilized on a stage, the carnival generates *pompe*, that is to say, procession, continuous movement, renewing dynamism of the world. It combines the *dran* of perpetual activity, the *orjeisthai* of rhythmic walking, and the *mimeisthai* that assumes the personality of the Other. The carnival, open-air theater of the agora and the marketplace, is both action and contemplation, actor and spectator, reciprocal and exchanged assumption of these roles.

The theater, and here I am referring, from the beginning, to the foundational or Greek theater, is the aesthetic dump of ancient festivals and rites of popular religiosity. As Rodríguez Adrados has said in his rich and dense book **Fiesta, comedia y tragedia**, "its themes of the Savior, the Rebel, peace and happiness, the *sophrosyne* and, at the same time, the license and the breaking of the limit, the impossible defeated and the Evil expelled or dead or cured, the laughter and the pain, are characteristics of the agrarian feast in general".

Let us now take a leap in time and go to the nascent 19th century in France. During the carnival celebrations in the countryside of that country, the theater, a timeless aesthetic, and magical fact preserves the heritage of the popular *agon.*

In this respect, Mademoiselle Pastor, questioned by Varagnac, says: "Disguised and masked, the boys imitated (or, moreover, *singeaient*) the healers, the rural mounted police, the gendarmerie, the sleepwalkers, the astrologers, the charlatans, the dentists; they spoiled the production of incredible foods, sold extraordinary objects, pronounced with a cavernous voice extravagant speeches, and improvised grotesque scenes".

This was popular art, peasant art of farce, that is to say, pure carnival. And if we want other examples, to think of the carnival prototypes embodied by the Italian **Commediadell'arte**, which included the medieval harlequins of the army of demons and the *pierrots* of the army of the dead would be enough.

THE CARNIVAL AS A FESTIVAL

Throughout the year, there are special days or periods marked by the sign of the celebration which are separated from the profanity of work and leisure. They are consecrated days which, while establishing a special type of time, impose a certain state on the spirits.

Carnival belongs to these festive periods. It is both Chaos and Golden Age: it evokes the foundation and beginning of things so that things do not rebel against man, as happened in the Chimú myth; it promotes momentary and regenerative disorder so that order may then prevail in the seasons and in societies. The carnivalesque intrusion into the gravity of human reason and the logic of nature turns the rules upside down.

The world looks at itself from behind the mirror. Categories, qualities, and estates are turned upside down. Sacred madness advances on the territory of sanity and annihilates when it opposes its path. It invites prolongation, calls to exaltation, and to debauchery. Dance, food, drink, and sex become, for a brief period, the masters of the world.

But things are not as they seem: the spoilage and excess appear as a sacrificial offering and not as blind destruction. At the end of the revelry and licenses of all kinds will appear the forces that, gathering the fragments of the maculated and shattered reality, will restore the form and meaning of everyday life by summoning again the utilitarian signs of profane time.

The carnival, from the underside of the social and ritual fabric, unloads its purifying paroxysm so that humanity may face, renewed and purged, the fatigue of work and the evening fire of homes and, by extension, the routine may reign in the rhythms of nature.

Attempts to bring order and balance to the suddenness and bustle of the carnival are vain and erroneous. Is there anything less carnival-like than the municipal parade of groups along Montevideo's 18 de Julio Avenue? There, the spirit of the festival has been lost: there is no crowd, no furious improvisation, no puns, no *agon* or *ilinx*.

It is a languid parade, insipid, municipal, and thick. It has been emptied of the frenetic and salvationist sense of a festival that is neither pagan nor Christian but a constant in the mythology of man as the inventor of his paradises and his hells. Whoever wants to study the function of the feast has at hand the texts of Kerenyi, Caillois, van der Leeuw, and

Cassirer. I refer to them, but not before insisting on the festive, that is, sacred accents of the carnival. The jester, after all, is only the messenger of a numen, the executor of a deity.

CARNIVAL AS A GAME

Carnival is **The Game** par excellence. It is the triumph of the "as if", the collective assumption of alternative, altered, and alienated social roles. Behind the mask, the face mask or the eye mask is consummated the multitudinous jubilee of mimicry, which is both mimesis and mimicry. The carnival allows the timid to become bold, the hypocrisy of daily coexistence to give way to the shameless and covert denunciation, and compliance with hierarchies to give way to merciless criticism.

That is why the carnival inaugurates the great open court of truth, the pillory that exhibits the unpunished, the moral scaffold that shows the dark side of power and wealth. Likewise, alterity also opens the doors to the domains of mystery: who am I? where do I come from? do you remember me? each of these phrases springs from anonymity, from the swamp of indeterminacy, from the I don't know what of doubt.

Other roles are the ultramundane: monsters, skulls, wandering spirits that finally take hold of the soul of the disguised and drive them mad with the hallucinogenic mushrooms of the Afterlife.

Along with the *mimicry* comes the vertigo, the *ilinx*. The frenetic rounds, the runs, the thunderous disorder, the hysterical shouting end up turning the masked into a possessed person who plays to the endless ecstasy, to the bacchic fury that does not extinguish. Games are also the singing of the troupe and murgas [street musicians], the sprinkling of water, the parade of the zoolatry mimics in the corsos--consult the dictionary about what corso primitively meant-- the frightening races of the giants and big-heads, the churning of men and animals, the promiscuous copulations, the absurd love affairs, the tongue twisters and the speeches, the universal imposition of madness. But this extreme forces us to a new unmasking: that of the carnival as an infatuation.

CARNIVAL AS INFATUATION

Infatuation is the exalted side of madness and melancholy is its depressive side. In the old carnival, that of the crowded streets, of the frenzied popular dances and the unbridled assaults on houses or people, the madness of excitement, the maenadic madness of the dance, the eloquent madness of the nonsensical speech prevailed.

It was a form of what psychologists call communicated madness: a collective delirium in which some incubi mobilized the madness of the succubus; and there were also cases of simultaneous madness in which, as Regis explains, the delirious ideas appear at the same time and expand by reciprocal interaction.

In 1789 Goethe published his famous article on the carnival in Rome. There he speaks of the drunkenness induced by the words and the "clamor of so many creatures that shout all the more the less they can boil", all of which causes "vertigo even to the most temperate".

For his part, Pedro de Repide, when he writes about the customs of Madrid at the beginning of this century, refers to the ceremony of the joint burial of the sardine and the carnival's wimp on Tuesday, the last day of the popular festival.

He says that "in the middle of an orgy, that had much of sabbatical, and at the glow of the bonfires where the papers were burning, the sardine was buried". Uttering "howls as of demons" the common people dressed "the most garish attire in the craziest masquerade".

Suddenly, already at the end of that scandal of lunatics, there was silence "to listen to the funeral prayers of the ceremony, which is made with the most grotesque gravity. For a moment, one hears burlesque chants and parodies of miseries that split the air like groans from beyond the grave. Then, the confusion of barbaric cries, of oaths and blasphemies, of brutal cooing and light couplets appear again. There are red stains on the garments of the masks, red with wine or blood. In the darkness of the night, like a witches' coven glow, the bonfires gleam their flames".

This is magic, infernal theater, delirious play, collective madness. This is, in short, or was, the spirit of the Shrovetide.

But this carnival madness does not agree with the one warned by Euripides: the gods previously madden to those they want to destroy. The Dionysian madness was exhausted in the sacred fury of the dance. During the carnival, on the other hand, the madness of the words that cannot and should not be uttered in the republic of conventions invades the area of silence that power imposes to conceal its sins and crimes.

This intrepid infatuation points then to the revelation of the evils that ferment in the Pandora's Box of the human spirit: the repressed truth, the silenced reason, the suffocated justice, come to light in the foolish and at the same time sane speech of the talking fool, of the indiscreet concealer, of the little song chanted by the wise and moralizing masks.

That, more than madness, is tolerated and ritual impertinence, a flash of divine light that clears the shadows of worldly hypocrisy. Infatuation stimulates social ethics and becomes a collective inquisition of sins and sinners. In the end, what began as a raving finishes as a license to liberate repressed thoughts and feelings. And what looks like madness is also therapy.

CARNIVAL AS THERAPY

The wildness of the party, the verboideological [dynamic discourse], and at the same time eloquent freedom of the theater, and the vertiginous circularity of the game constitute a form of magic. This collective magic has the virtue of restoring health after madness.

It is a magic that summons the *katharsis*, that is to say, the purging and purification of the spirits; that works as a *pharmacon* or medicine; that propitiates the *alexicacos,* that is to say, the distancing of the evil.

The carnival, Gordian knot of multiple ceremonies of liberation and restitution, was originally a therapeutic celebration. Its outburst of momentary madness cured the neurasthenia caused by weeks and months of imposed conventions and forced compliance.

The three days of drunkenness, statutory sex, role reversals, symbolic masquerades, agitations, fantasies, and mysteries made up a multitudinous healing of burdens and routines. It liberated morbidities and bet on balance by way of excess. In short, it liberated by derivation, as psychiatrists say.

This ancient and salutary function has been lost. Other institutions of the State or official religions have reclaimed it in the name of modernization and rationalization of society.

The contemporary world, regulated and planned, no longer has room for carnival. What we call carnival today, here, in Rio de Janeiro or in any other country in the world, is just a dysfunctional parody of what used to be, splendidly, the strategy for restoring popular health.

The entire Western society has been in crisis, it is said, for a century now. But carnival is also a crisis, and as such we must consider it.

CARNIVAL AS CRISIS

Crisis means change and nothing else. Carnival, in that sense, is a critical period. The poor are allowed to denigrate the rich and history tells us that the nobles, in disguise, took to the streets to scourge the poor. This is change, a crisis in the best meaning of the word.

But what is common to the carnival is the reversal of roles. It is the inversion of the binary semiotic oppositions studied by M. Bakhtin: male-female, poor-rich, prince- beggar, free-slave, ugly-pretty. These oppositions do not refer to a dialectical future but to a mythical past where an equality of conditions and sexes alluded to the indeterminacy of an androgynous and undifferentiated world, even before the Golden Age.

It would be, in short, the atavistic evocation of the cosmic and social egg from which creatures and their shadows, the concurrence and divergence of life, would be born. The struggle between ritual and myth analyzed by structuralist anthropologists is revealed in the transmutations of the carnival, in its infatuations and festivities, in its orchestration, and its theatrical dalliances.

To explain these mechanisms would be complex and perhaps boring. It is enough to point them out. In order not to remain in the bare bones of theory, nothing would be better than to revive the expressive cultural history of the carnivals in America and Uruguay, today turned into relics or ghosts, if not in counters and shop windows. But that is enough for now.

THE LIVING EARTH

FROM THE GREAT ANIMAL TO THE HYPOTHESIS OF GAIA

Life as exercise or as spectacle, life as the physical presence or as metaphysical essence, life as cozy intimacy of the **I** or as a pertaining threatening of the **Other**, life as existential neatness or as human misery, life as an adventure of being in space or as the expiration of the appearing in time, life, in short, as a provisional, though privileged, condition of matter, or as a vigilant and creative, though not always noticed, activity of the spirit, proposes the most eminent of those themes whose coming and going along the daily path of the colloquial or the solemn and often conceited air of academic discourse, has turned them into tarnished topics, in the levels of banality.

ZOON AND BIOS

The Greeks had already noticed that the vital phenomenon had two faces. One was the *thymós*, that impulse that energizes and alerts the corporeal system of plants and animals, whose correspondent in the human order, the soul, the *psyché*, adds the superior condition of rational thought to the double grace of movement and sensibility. The human soul is a breath, an *anima*, as the Romans called it, which, in the same way as

93

the Greek *psyché*, flees from the body at the moment of death. But it is also the *animus*, the motor of the understanding and the spirit. Both in the order of the *thymós*, which from the animating principle of *lahylé*, matter, becomes, by metaphorical transposition, a valiant will to power and in that of the *psyché*, one is in the domain of life as *zoon*. The *zoon*, thus considered, exhibits itself in all its splendor in that marvelous sphere of life, the biosphere, which has clothed the body of the world with a colorful variety of creatures. One million species have been identified among insects, although entomologists believe that in a few decades this figure will at least double. There are eighty thousand species of mollusks, almost thirty thousand of worms, and twenty thousand of fish. Birds number nine thousand, reptiles and amphibians exceed six thousand, and mammals, where, in the order of primates, the proud *Homo sapiens* claims to be the highest in ranking, number around six thousand. This fantastic array of animal species is set against the backdrop of some four hundred thousand species of chlorophyll plants with which the populations of consumers have immediate or mediate trophic relationships. However, the above figure, according to the galloping pace of current research, will increase significantly. Indeed, botanists are annually adding to this inventory more than four thousand species, and what about the world of bacteria, fungi, diatoms, algae, whose species may triple the number resulting from the sum of plant and animal species? This is what is today called biodiversity and which, thanks to the old semantic concept, should be called zoo-diversity. With the passing of time, zoology has been limited to the study of animals; botany, from the Greek *botanós*, plant, has claimed for several centuries the description of the vegetal kingdom.

The other conception of life among the Greeks referred to the practical activity of men, to the sociability exercised in the *polis*, the anthropic space par excellence. There, in the agora, in the open air, *nomos*, that is, convention as local custom, established scales of values circumscribed to a given environment and time. From the social *nomos* springs the philosophical nominalism, the relativized truth, or, if you will, humanized truth. This represented the understanding of the sophists, whose vindication by Hegel, after a long exile, reinstated them in their eminent role in the history of thought.

This activity understood as *bios*, turns *zoon* into *politikon*, if it is a question of man, for it is in the city that the essential characteristic of humanity, that is, civilization, which is equivalent to the politicization of consciousness (civility) and the refinement of models (urbanity), reaches its highest degree.

In short, *zoon* is life understood as the feature that is common to certain types of animate beings; *bios*, on the other hand, is what the communal existence of men adds, or rather, superimposes, to the purely zoological. This means that there is a level, transcendent according to some or simply prospective according to others -it does not matter--, to which the sedentary existence of the plant and the roving existence of the animal have not yet had access: that of the axiological categories, that of the duty to be as a prescription or as salvation, that of the criterion for discerning between the good and the bad, between the just and the unjust, and between the ugly and the pretty. This evaluative capacity, projected to the theater of human actions, is transformed into conduct, ethics, movement, or simply moral life.

Nowadays, the fine nuance established by that double significance of the living has been lost. The biotic and the biological encompass what formerly corresponded to the *zoon* and the zoological, although, in compensation, contemporary science and philosophy have been in charge of enriching and/or complexifying the *denotata* included by those terms.

"Our Lives Are the Rivers/That End Up in the Sea/Which Represents Dying..."

We cannot, in any case, renounce to the presence and urgency of themes and problems that accompany us throughout our existence as the shell to the snails: whether we want or not, we carry them all the time, and many times after hours, on our backs and our thoughts. Whenever we want to hide them or distort them, they are in charge of making us wake up, sometimes shouting, from the momentary oblivion. Thus, between tugging, between chimeras, escapes, and reveries, each singular man as a person becomes a gambler who, during his residence on Earth, plays a game of dice with death until the latter wins the last hand.

This playful activity, marked by the double sign of the Heideggerian "cure" on the one hand and the randomness of circumstances on the other, to which is added the expiration inherent to every human creature, has made it possible to develop, together with existence, perpetuated throughout the lower asymptote of the species, a personal consciousness that registers and at the same time symbolizes, by fabricating all kinds of tropes, the struggle that has been waged between two great cosmic moments since the very beginning of things.

These solemn as well as dramatic moments, considered by various theologies and mythologies as the ebb and flow of successive creations and extinctions, are, on the one hand, the genetic activities, sentient and in certain cases culturizing activity of living beings, which ceaselessly diversifies and disseminates on the surface of the globe to millions of creatures endowed with different degrees of psychism and innate capacity for reproduction and, on the other, the implacable annihilation of such organisms and skills at the end of their vital parabola.

The alternating rhythm between life and death is equally fulfilled on our Earth and in the Universe of which we are a part. And so powerful is the impact of the biotic in our minds, heirs at last of old animistic beliefs, that we grant the cosmic energy, "the entelechy of what is in potency", as Aristotle defined the movement, the meaning of a kind of life that animates the evolution of the stars and the flight of the galaxies. Thus we speak of the "birth" of the worlds and the thermal "death" of the Universe. This animistic treatment of the (supposedly) inorganic realm reveals the persistence of remote conceptions that underlie the aseptic waters of scientific theory and that, as such, resist the idea of a sterile, mineral, pascal Cosmos, condemned to the final abdication of light, to the ominous empire of dust, to the voracity of black holes.

A distinction must be made, however, between the creative art which with a divine breath animates matter -- the low, the formless, the imperfect, the malignant, as the Neoplatonic conception considered it -- and the self-sufficiency of the organic system, to which a series of efficient causes, products of necessity and chance and not of the tinkering of Providence, wind it up and thus set it in motion. In the first case, the explanation of vitalism operates, and in the second, mechanism is in use. Both philosophical positions, since very far back in the history of thought, have tried to explain, refuting reciprocally their basic theses, the phenomena of life.

But let us stop here: whoever asks, once again, about the ultimate nature of life, will have to review the variety of answers born to mitigate the millenary sting caused by that question in the mortal beings who call themselves men, that is, humble as humus. These men have always humbled their heads in the dust before the majesty of the *mysterium tremens et fascinans* of the sacred.

THE BIOTIZATION OF THE COSMOS

Now it is a question of entering into the heart of a matter not so transcendent but no less curious. In this way, I will relate the conception that considered the world as a great sentient and intelligent animal, typical of animistic, magical, and mythical imaginations, with the hypothesis of a living Earth that regulates the world's climate. This is none other than the hypothesis of Gaia, the ancient goddess who nowadays, desacralized, continues to create the favorable conditions of her environmental habitat through the creation and regulation of a thermal diapason that makes all the climates of the world favorable to all manifestations of terrestrial life, that is, life that develops on land and in water. The hypothesis of Gaia, which undoubtedly has a metaphysical and, if we hurry things, even mythical background, has been handled, by means of a not inconsiderable biological and mathematical foundation, by two contemporary scientists.

The comparison between the two extremes seems rash. But as soon as we approach the paradigmatic plot of both models, the archaic and the current one, we will be able to verify that the gulf opened between science and the bundle of explanations, so-called irrational, fabulous, and prelogical, managed, between whispers and concealments, by that which is called Tradition[7], is not so insurmountable.

---

[7] On the Tradition - which we must understand as Hermetic tradition - consult the renowned books of René Guénon (Introductiongénérale à l'étude des doctrines hindoues, 1921; Orient et Occident, 1924; La

This idea of the biotization of the Cosmos, sustained by this tradition, is common to the cosmovision of the Eastern initiates adopted by the West and to the organicist doctrines of some present-day scientists, including Von Bertalanffy[8]. This vision, on the other hand, is part of a series of interrelated re-evolutions (re-evolution means to return, after a circular trajectory, to the starting point), such as the *kitra* era and the *kali* era of Hindustani cosmology, the back and forth between yin (the masculine Heaven) and yang (the feminine Earth) of Chinese thought, the cyclical predominance of the even and odd numbers of Pythagorean numerology and, despite the bridge that leads to the human, the *corsi e ricorsi* of Giambattista Vico or the organicist and recurrent conception of history of Oswald Spengler.

Somehow all these circular conceptions of the Universe and life, some of them born in the Neolithic or even earlier, become like the archives of the infused philosophy of the *Homo* species. This "unwritten philosophy", the one supposed by the people, the one accepted by "everybody", as Cornford, a historian of ancient philosophy, explains with great clarity, has always given ample credit to the notions that, with greater refinement, have been elaborated by the occult doctrines. Such doctrines, far more pertinent and important than the disbelieving scientific society can imagine, constitute the *basso continuo* which, beginning with Hermes Trismegistus, or "thrice

---

crise du monde moderne, 1927; La metaphysiqueorientale, 1939; L'esoterismechrétien, 1951; Symbolesfondamentaux de la sciencesacrée, 1962). Also of interest is the work of Julius Evola, in particular La tradición hermética, Martínez Roca, Barcelona, 1975

[8] Ludwig von Bertalanffy. Biological Conception of the Cosmos. Universidad de Chile, Santiago, 1963.

great," runs through the temporal expressions, always faithful to the teaching of the Ancients, of Western Hermeticism[9].

The confrontation between light and shadow, between the cradle and the coffin, between the youth that gives wings to life and the old age that spins the cocoon of death, between the cry of the newborn and the hiccups of the dying old man, between the fleetingness of human existence and the apotheosis of mourning, etc. was made a metaphor, century after century, by the elegiac voice of the poets. Indeed, one is always reminded of Horace's First Ode, Villon, Manrique, Ronsard, and forgotten among so many others - the alienation of the American soul began with the trauma of the conquest - the disconsolate lamentations of the Aztecs during the siege of Tenochtitlan. But this confrontation between life and death was also mathematized by physicists and biologists who, through equations, consider it as a quantifiable arm-wrestling match between entropy and negentropy, between the Second Law of Thermodynamics and diectopy, between funerary objects and epictesis, as Hellenized, with its hidden cryptic nomination, by the language of science, thus converted into the secularized vehicle of a new hermeticism.

PRELIMINARY NOTION ABOUT THE BIOSPHERE

The immensity of the subject obliges us to choose only one aspect of it. This choice, in this case, will be limited to the current concept of the biosphere, a macro-entity which, the

---

[9] Classics on this are: A.J. Feshugière. **La Révélationd'HérmesTrimegiste**. Les BellesLettres, Paris, 1950-54 (four volumes) y **Corpus Hermeticum**, Les BellesLettres, Paris, 1945 (four volumes).

more it is studied, reveals a singular kinship between the notions of the Great Archaic Knowledge kept in their memory by the different communities of the world and the recent proposals of scientific knowledge.

The biosphere is the sphere of life. Our planet, and what goes below our feet and above our heads, has been divided into a series of superimposed concentric spheres that follow one another like the layers of a gigantic onion. Geologists and geographers thus speak of a **nucleosphere**, or **nife**, where, at great pressures and thousands of degrees of temperature, nickel (Ni) and iron (Fe) predominate, melted in a flask that heats the Devil's own eternal flame, as the traditional demonologies tell us. This central core, in turn, is covered by an **asthenosphere** (weak, soft, plastic sphere) or **barysphere** (deep sphere) made up of very dense and heavy rocks still bubbling with metals. On top of these rocks, real subterranean frameworks built by the bones, tendons, and muscles of the Earth's powerful body, a crust of stone and lighter materials, called lithosphere (stone sphere), extends like skin. This lithosphere, which averages seventy kilometers thick, is made of increasingly lighter rocks as one ascends to the surface of the globe. The upper discontinuity consists of two parts: one, the **chasm** - silica (Si) and magnesium (Ma) - as designated by Süss, also the inventor of the above acronym, consists of a continuous envelope of basalts. This rocky mantle can be compared to an ocean sailed by the enormous granite rafts of **sial** - silica (Si) and aluminum (Al) - where the continents sail. These colossal fragments, broken off from a Pangaea during its drift from east to west, as anticipated by Wegener at the beginning of the century and later confirmed by plate tectonics, support, not without risk to life and the technogenic fabric, the settlement of man and his works.

The **lithosphere** is in contact with two other spheres, with which it engages in a subtle series of relationships and interfaces. One of these is the **hydrosphere**, the sphere of water, and the **atmosphere**, the sphere of air, which, if we were to be faithful to etymology, would have to be changed to the sphere of vapor since, in Greek, *atmós* means that and nothing else. The water and the air enter the superficial chinks of the earth, hydrogenating and oxidizing it; the earth flies in the breath of the winds and is carried by the rivers towards the belly of the seas, where it is deposited and sediments; the air enters the water and the earth itself, taking advantage, in the latter case, besides the vertical tunnels opened by worms, of the cracks and pores of the rough epidermis of the former; The water, converted into steam, is integrated into the atmosphere or boils in the deep cauldrons of the planet where the "geothermal degree" increases as one descends towards the interior where high temperatures and increasing densities prevail.

In this complex and osmotic scenario where water, air, and land converge is where life appeared and developed, evolving and diversifying for over four billion years until it perfected the **biosphere,** as it appears today, on the face of the world. This biosphere is, at the same time, a dialectical entity, a cybernetic ingenuity (or engineer), and a consistory of alchemists: its manipulations, multiple and complicated, despite its essential simplicity, created the air we breathe from the oxygen produced by oceanic phytoplankton and subsequent terrestrial plants.

Indeed, for life to emerge from the sea, where it initially appeared in a medium of warm, slightly salty water, equal in its sodium chloride content to our blood, it was necessary to form, from the oxygen expanded from the ocean prairies, the ozone shield (O_3) that protected the colonizers of the continents from the lethal burn of ultraviolet and infrared rays. And once the plants occupied the land, all the chlorophyll flora of

102

the planet, added to that of the prairies of the sea, began to transform the carbon dioxide of the lower atmosphere into carbohydrates, releasing oxygen, which, used by the animals in their respiration, allowed the return of carbon dioxide to the universal air, thus closing one of the many cycles of this workshop of life. The plants once settled in the earth, created the **pedosphere**, the deep soils, and the **homosphere**, the superficial mulch. In short, the death of plants and associated animals in ecosystem communities, by converting the graves into life-supporting beds, contributes to the creation of an environment favorable to all possible future biota.

Living matter forms biomass. This has a weight that has been calculated, without agreeing on its numbers, by ecologists; notwithstanding its astronomical figure of millions of tons and cubic kilometers, if it were converted into a paste and then spread over the surface of the globe -- five hundred and ten million square kilometers -- it would not exceed two centimeters in height. Such biomass, even if it grows, cannot increase the total weight of our planet as has sometimes been said, with more horror than error, to be the case. It simply remains in equilibrium with the other materials that make up the Earth -- "nothing is created, nothing is destroyed..." -- because our world is a closed system in the order of matter, although open in the order of energy coming, almost exclusively, from the heat and light of the Sun.

In addition to constituting the living matter, proper of the biomass that here and now expresses itself in multiple terrestrial and aquatic biomes, life, as Vernadsky pointed out in the 1920s, appears as the perpetual genitor of **biogenic** matter and as the building partner of **biocosmic** matter.

Biogenic matter has its origin in the life of the past. It is mineralized, petrified, encapsulated life which, however, has not lost its former potency: apparently dead, it retains its caloric and luminous capacity. Indeed, the solar energy received by the Earth during the primary era, which was once processed by the chlorophyll function, is ensiled in the coal deposits. These are reservoirs of solar heat, whose dormant potentiality was conserved in the batteries manufactured by the flora after an ancient physicochemical process. But the organic matter of the past is not only found in the underground cellars of anthracite and hard coal. The lignite of the tertiary era as well as peat, combustible gases, bitumen, and sapropel - sediment formed underwater from the putrid remains of plants and animals - are all direct offspring of life.

Biocosmic matter has life as co-author. Water from plant evapotraspiration and animal ejections is added to that released by decomposing bodies; the breathable air that forms part of the lower atmosphere or troposphere is generated in part by the respiration of flora and fauna, in which we humans are included. To these two elements the presence of life in sedimentary rocks and clays, in the case of the mineral world is added. A marble, a metamorphic rock, originates from slow thermal and mechanical processes imposed on limestone deposits, which, in turn, are made up of fossilized remains of coelenterates and mollusks. Thus, marble becomes a grandchild, if the term fits, of life itself.

Plant populations, made up of primary producers, complete, self-sufficient beings, or **autotrophs**, as ecologists call them, feed the first-degree consumers, the herbivores - whether terrestrial or aquatic - and these, in turn, feed the carnivores, second-, third- and even fourth-degree consumers. But here is the revenge of the Second Law of Thermodynamics: since one cannot return to pick up what was lost on the way, the process of the metabolic chain is fulfilled by an inevitable loss of heat in each of its links. On the other hand, the law of 10% is firmly established: 100 kilograms of plant biomass is converted into 10 kilograms of herbivorous animal

104

biomass and one kilogram of carnivorous animal biomass. In turn, this kilogram is reduced to 100 grams in the case of secondary carnivores and to 10 grams in the case of tertiary carnivores. The chain of **phagotrophe**, then, goes like this, just as an example and if we limit ourselves to what happens in the open air and not underwater: antelopes, lion, hyena, eagle.

BIOSPHERE AND NECROSPHERE, OR THE HARMONY OF OPPOSITES.

The offal of all of them, the devoured and the devourers, once the living matter, organized by life, has been converted into biogenic matter, disorganized by death, are attacked by saprotrophs, decomposers, and reducers. These invisible chemicals--bacteria, fungi, scavenging microorganisms, which act like tiny vultures--allegedly swoop down on the corpses of plants and animals, corrupting them, disintegrating them, returning the waters to the waters, the gases to the air, and the minerals to the solid and aquatic environments from which they came. The **microbiota** thus closes, like the uroboros of the alchemists, the circle of trophic or alimentary mutations, microcosmic samples of the Eternal Return.

This is even more complicated because of the presence of the Sun and the chlorophyll activity of the plant and the digestive activity of the animal, by animating the metabolic processes of the producing and transforming organisms, at the beginning of the chain, and the quasi-magical activity of the microbiota, at the end of it, lead us to the cybernetic domain of the proper administration of energy. The determined uphill climb, thanks to the loops of retroactive information - by means of a homeostatic plate - courageously confronts the arrow of time, says "not yet" to the universal arrogance of entropy, and engages in a pathetic and at the same time admirable duel against the universal degradation of energy. Life moves millions of tons of minerals, water, and gases through the constant migration of atoms triggered precisely by the biotization of the **lithosphere**, the **hydrosphere,** and the **atmosphere**. In such a way, the matter is recycled by the unidirectional flow of energy, which, in turn, is partially recaptured and reconverted ("stop for a brief minute, how beautiful you are") thanks to the trigger of retroaction. Such retroaction is propitiated by a computer agenda that becomes the foresighted and attentive cybernetic helmsman of every biotic system. In such a way, the mentioned mechanisms, acting with different rhythms, succeed in making every living entity resist to the maximum the onslaught of death at the same time that they transfer to the species the virtue of enduring the stubborn, but finally defeated, diecotropic resistance of the individual beings.

Consider the above as a brief introduction to the dynamics of the biosphere. Much more should be said about the teleological objectives pursued by the admirable activity of ecosystems, organisms, and cells. These cells are the ultimate protagonists of the drama of survival. But let the above outline serve as a minimum threshold so that, when we set foot on it, what is written below has an intelligible basis.

THE MUSIC OF THE SPHERES

The "spheres" described so far, that the process of hominization initiated three or four million years ago complemented and completed - at least we believe so - with the revolutionary irruption of the **anthroposphere** and the **technosphere,** are the ones that scientific thought considers as the only ones worthy of being taken into account. In doing so, the other spheres have been abolished, half astronomical, half theological, which, from the Middle Ages onwards, indebted in turn to classical antiquity - Aristotle and Ptolemy, principally - constituted the colossal architecture that was deployed on the basis of a geocentric conception of the universe.

Science kills the myth, puts an end to the imagination and the imagery of the fantastic, assassinates the choreography of the tiny angels that danced on the heads of the pins. It is said that it has been for the best, that the equations are full of beauty and poetry, that epistemological clarity has dispelled the shadows of superstition and ignorance. Let us admit that this is so. Electronic music has silenced the music of the spheres, and the earthly spheres, claimed by geologists as mere objects of knowledge, have condemned the celestial spheres and angelic hierarchies to discredit and oblivion.

Nevertheless, it is worth remembering them, even as a paragraph in the history of thought.

The cosmic model of the Middle Ages was more complete than ours or, at least, possessed the grace of the transcendent. Our terrestrial sphere, home to mankind, animals, plants, and the elements, constituted the center of the *Natura naturata* situated in the sublunary world. This world, in turn, was composed of the successive spheres of Earth, Water, Air and Fire, the purest of the elements, the one that poor Quixote, the plaything of the cruel Dukes, though he could guess when, blindfolded, he rode the Clavileño, the stick horse, on his imaginary journey to the highest heavens.

With the Fire sphere ended, the sublunar sphere, and above it, each governed by the respective angelic intelligence, were, in concentric arrangement, the spheres of the Moon, Mercury, Venus, the Sun, Mars, Jupiter, Saturn, and the fixed stars. When rotating from east to west around the Earth, these spheres, which move at different speeds, rubbed against each other, and the celestial music that comes from this rubbing was then produced. The heavens also have their limit: this is the *Primun Mobile*, the first engine that every twenty-four hours closes a race that goes from the west to the east, starting the underlying spheres in the opposite direction to its own.

There still remains a Third Dominion, a Third and Sacred sphere. But this superior stratum, which finishes and completes the structure that begins in the deep metallic pit of our earthly home, is outside Nature. It is the Empyrean, the House of God, that is to say, a realm without beginning, without end, without boundaries in space and time, to which, after the Final Judgment, the souls of the blessed will travel to sing eternal praises to the glory of the Lord.

THE GREAT ANIMAL AND THE SOUL OF THE WORLD

The concept of the **biosphere**, defined on the basis of the concentric circles that myth, metaphysics, magic, alchemy, and theology trace around the central nucleus of science, becomes an inciting motive to attempt, in the light of the new paradigms - especially that of the general theory of systems, which encompasses the homeostatic behavior of biosystems - a series of reflections, as will be immediately presented in these pages.

The **biosphere**, as described above, constitutes the living part of our planet. It forms a kind of thin superficial skin stretched irregularly over the body of the Earth, which the ancients imagined as a Great Animal. This animated entity in

108

perpetual wakefulness, which the Greeks not only considered as sentient and thinking, was endowed by Plato, in that enigmatic dialogue which is the Latin **Timaeus**, with a *megalépsyché*, whose Latin equivalent is the *Anima Mundi.* The term, when incorporated into Western philosophy, was transformed, according to the idiomatic varieties, into the Soul of the World, *World-Soul, Weltseele, Âme du Monde*, etc.

Our earthly dwelling, as a living being, whose bones are represented by the minerals, its flesh by the components of the soil, its veins and arteries by the rivers and the tempestuous contents of the pelvic cavity by the waters and winds of the sea, constituted a privileged object in the meditation of the pre-Socratic philosophers. According to Thales of Miletus, who made water the primordial *arjé* of all things, the world was full of gods. By professing a **hylozoism** of this type (matter is a living being) the pre-Socratic sage -- who, considering it from another point of view, culminates the period of *mythos* and replaces it with that of *logos* -- reasoned in the same way as the animists and pre-learned animists of antiquity[10] and the "savage" peoples of the contemporary age[11].

Anaxagoras, who attributed to the *Nous* the faculty of setting the whole Cosmos in motion, took a step forward, for he separated the animator from the animate. Centuries later, the Stoic Posidonius, who had considered man as a microcosm, returned to the archaic sources by supposing the existence of a true universal metabolism, including in it the **anabolic** and **catabolic** phases. This process turned the Cosmos

---

[10] The difference between animatism and animism is analyzed by Nataniel Mickelm, Religion, Oxford University Press, London, 1948.

[11] Etymologically savage, from the Portuguese selvagem, means man of the jungle. Value judgments added pejorative meanings to the original word, a mere toponym.

into a living organism, whose parts were intimately interrelated. Throughout the different phases of the Stoic school, to which this thinker belonged, the idea of the Cosmos as "an immortal, rational, perfect, and intelligent animal in its happiness, incapable of receiving any harm" had been refined, confusing it with God properly speaking. God was the Cosmos and the Cosmos was God. It is impossible to find a more complete conception of pantheism: God thus appears as the **spermatic logos,** as the seminal reason of the world. In explaining this curious approach, Diogenes Laertius adds that "they call world... to God, who is the very quality of all substance, immortal and unbegotten, creator of the universal order, who according to the cycles of time absorbs into himself all substance, consuming it and begetting it anew from himself"[12]. Matter is the passive and God is active, but this activity presupposes heat, the exhilarating fire, in short, the Sun: this is how the "primitives" had already conceived it, for whom **sunshine duration** was confused with **theophania**. And it is not only the "primitives" - an improper word, if there is one - who confer the supreme dignity on the father Sun: from the **Horus** of the Egyptians, who illuminated the waters of the Nile every morning with his flaming falcon, to the **Inti** of the Andean Aborigines, the Sun, warm and fertile artisan of life, dispenser of light and joy among mortals, played the role of father grower of the crops. The one capable of performing these miracles can be none other than a God.

In the same way, the Stoics, anticipating the laws of thermodynamics, affirmed that "everything that lives, be it animal or plant, lives by the heat contained in it. From which it follows that the nature of heat has in itself a vital force which is diffused throughout the world... All parts of the world, then, are sustained by heat... and the world itself is preserved in such

---

[12] Diógenes Laercio. **Vidas, opiniones y sentencias de los filósofos más ilustres**. El Ateneo, Buenos Aires, 1947.

a long duration by a similar and equal nature, and it must be understood that this heat and this fire is thus interpenetrated with all nature, that inside it is the force of all procreation and the cause of all birth"[13].

The idea of the Soul of the World was also in force among the Neoplatonists who established a trinity, allying Christian theology with philosophy. This Trinity was organized as follows: the Father was the *Mens*, the son, the *Intellectus*, and the Spirit, the *Anima Universalis*. Christianity, which perfectly separated the contingency of the Created from the eternity of the Creator, thus dispelling the pantheistic confusion, nevertheless accepted the idea of the Soul of the World by some figures of medieval scholasticism. Abelard, in this sense, equated it with the Holy Spirit.

These antecedents prefigure the later developments that will be manifested in almost all the thinkers of the Italian Renaissance (especially Giordano Bruno), given to magical practices[14], and in the doctrines of the alchemists. They believed that all of nature was animated. Thus, stones and metals grow and mature like plants in the bosom of the Earth. The heat of the sun in tropical zones, added to the heat that comes from the bowels of the world, generates metals, and therefore those considered precious, given their scarcity and beauty. That is why Columbus sought in the warm regions of the Antilles the marvelous regions where "gold is born". The alchemist assumes that matter, besides spontaneously engendering matter and transmuting itself into another according to certain rules, has psychism. It is animated, sentient, and somehow able to think.

---

[13] Cicerón, **De Natura deorum. De la Nature des Dieux**. Librairie-GarnierFrères, Paris, 1935.

[14] Giordano Bruno. **De la causa, principio y uno**. Editorial Losada, Buenos Aires, 1941; Frances A. Yates. **Giordano Bruno y la Tradición Hermética**. Ariel, Barcelona, 1983.

There is no real separation between the organic and the inorganic, which implies, moreover, that the living and the dead are not so far apart as the profane vulgar suppose. In the alembic, the spirits of things are inflamed, the alcohols fly and expand, iridescent genii dance in retorts and illuminate them with mysterious interior lightning. Salt is the *corpus*; mercury, the *spiritu*; sulfur, the *anima*. Everything is related to each other, empathetically and sympathetically. **Microcosm** and **macrocosm** correspond, to the point that an alchemist, before beginning his work in the laboratory, consults the opinion of the stars.[15]

According to Paracelsus, vital processes develop in nature whose own essence cannot turn back the current of time. This concept foreshadows the entropic arrow. But what is really interesting is the cosmogony and theogony devised by this singular character, half doctor, half sorcerer. First of all, wrote the German occultist, there was the *ylliaster*, the *protomatter* not yet touched by the Creation, the prima *materiaomniumrerum*. Then comes chaos, the *mysteriummagnum*, when inanimate matter is penetrated by the spirit that permeates and mobilizes it. For its part, "the *mysteriummagno* has been the mother of all the elements (the four sensible elements are air, water, fire, and earth) and in them has become the grandmother of all the stars, the trees and the creatures of flesh and blood. Just like children are born from a mother, all beings, sentient and insentient, have been born from the great mystery. Once formed, they will not be repeated, for just as cheese never becomes milk again, generation does not return to its raw material". Degraded energy is not recomposed, although

---

[15] Among the multiple studies about alchemy and alchemists, and in addition to the classic by E.J. Holmyard, **Alchemy**, PelicanBooks, London 1956, see F. SherwoodShepard. **Los alquimistas**, Fondo de Cultura Económica, México 1975 and Titus Burchkardt, **Alquimia**, Plaza y Janés, Barcelona, 1972.

112

God, in the course of evolution -- Paracelsus does not speak of it, nor could he, but the concept pervades the discourse -- "has polished, corrected and raised things to the highest level: the later, the more so". (Does this not anticipate the later doctrine of incessant human progress, developed in the 18th century by Condorcet?).

Life, according to Paracelsus, is situated between prime matter and ultimate matter. Life is the *archeus*, the archeus, the ancient breath that gives animation to things, that detaches them from the initial *ylliaster*, that individualizes them and places within each one of them an own and non-transferable germ: "*archeusestista vis quæprodxit res, id estdispensator et compositor omniunrerum*". Thus, each being and each organism possesses a particular *ares*, a *spirituvitæ* that acts as a consummate alchemist. And this organism develops in an environment that is propitious or deadly, as the case may be. Sympathy and antipathy govern the processes of adaptation to the environment, which either benefit or annihilate.[16]

Anticipating the contemporary ecologist, Parecelsus foresees what happens within biosystems, where the dialectics with the favorable or adverse factors of climate, soil, and catastrophic changes imposed by nature or by man.

This mention of the biosystem, which becomes an ecosystem when studied from the energetic point of view, places us squarely on our subject, that is, the living nature of the ecosphere or biosphere, an entity not yet independent of the thought of magical thinking and the metaphysical inertias of a tenacious vitalism. Even today, the Earth continues to be compared to a great animate being, as is evident from the

---

[16] Honorio Delgado. **Paracelso**. Editorial Losada, Buenos Aires, 1947; Alexandre Koyré. **Místicos, espirituales y alquimistas del siglo XVI alemán**. Akal Editor, Barcelona, 1981, Cap. 3, Paracelso

examples, some of them nonsensical and others worthy of careful consideration, which I will cite immediately.

The first belongs to a police officer of Montauban, France, Lieutenant Chevrel-Dessaudrais, who, in 1805, published a book with a surprising title: **Key to the Phenomena of Nature or the Living Earth**.

What did this inventive local man say in his, sometimes hilarious, work? We learn from it, as expressed in an amusing summary written in our days, "that our globe is a gigantic animal, on whose back we live as parasites, like fleas on a skull. In fact, he could not tell whether we were in the presence of one or two separate animals. Different indications led him to think that the New World was the female of the Old World... Single animal or couple, the fact is that our Earth lives. It does not move in its orbit by virtue of universal gravitation, but by a movement of its own, like an animate being: it walks in the sky. Nevertheless, the reader will say, an animal needs to sleep. Chevrel-Dessaudrais believes, indeed, that the Earth sleeps during the winter months. Since it continues to move during that time, there is only one explanation: the Earth sleepwalks. The animate nature of the Earth is demonstrated by life itself. The support of life can only be alive; nothing grows in a dead body. If life were not common to Earth and animals, where would this similarity between the growth of grass and our beard come from? Another proof that our planet lives: we see it breathe. Tides cannot be explained in any other way. The regions of strong tides correspond to the animal's rib cage. What does the Earth feed on? With the same as the fish: with the bodies suspended in the water of the sea. Our unhappy Earth can even get sick. Then convulsions come to it: these are the earthquakes. As for the members of the animal, it is possible that they are folded under him. They are, therefore, submerged in the bottom of the oceans; but sometimes it moves them to wake up, then they are produced... the tidal waves. That is to say, the Earth lives".[17]

Between this crazy assumption and the theory of Dr. Jawosky, who in 1937 published a book about **Le Géonou la Terre vivante**, there is a difference of scholarship: both move in the territory of the absurd, but the crazy academic improve the language and refines the similes. The Geon is constituted by the living fabric of the **geosphere**, the **hydrosphere**, the **lithosphere**, the **zoosphere,** and the **anthroposphere**. Man does not live on the Earth; he lives with the Earth, as part of the shared life that animates our planet. The Earth is a gigantic cell: the nucleus of the interior is the heart, the protoplasm is constituted by the **atmosphere** and the **hydrosphere**, the membrane that covers it is nothing other than the **lithosphere**. The heart of the Geon pumps its blood to the entire body of the Great Animal. The central core, I say, cordially, sends waves of heat towards the surface, it is, simply, the circulation of the blood. If a volcanic eruption spills lava, we are dealing with a hemorrhage; when the lava cools in the form of gigantic heaps, the blood coagulates on the surface of the planet. The skeleton of the enormous terrestrial body is formed by rocks and mountain ranges: more than a skeleton, it resembles a chitinous covering and the Great Animal, although the author does not expressly say so, thus became an immense cockroach or coleopteran, as one prefers to say. The surface and subterranean waters make up the lymphatic system of this being and when the rivers flow out of the mother and the lagoons overflow, we are before a pathological manifestation: it is a simple and habitual edema. The whole humanity constitutes the grouping of nerve cells that give origin to the brain of this superbeing: the matrix phenomena are defined in the left cerebral hemisphere,

---

[17] François Derrey. **La Tierra, esa desconocida**. Editorial Sudamericana, Buenos Aires, 1969.

corresponding to the Americas, while Dr. Jawosky, a good European at last, reserves the right hemisphere, center of the intelligence and the language, to the Eurasian continent. This Great Animal is fed, otherwise, it would not be able to live. The daily nourishment is provided by the radiation of the father Sun. The nonsense goes on so that what we have seen so far is enough. But no one can deny that the old models elaborated by mythology, magic, and alchemy resound, like a tam-tam in the background, in the delusions of pseudoscientific charlatanism[18].

THE WORLD OF DAISIES

The Gaia hypothesis was pioneered by the joint work of microbiologist Lynn Margulis and atmospheric chemist James Lovelock but it is named after novelist William Golding. "The Gaia hypothesis is a theory of the atmosphere and surface sediments of planet Earth considered as a whole. The Gaia hypothesis in its most general form states that the temperature and composition of the Earth's atmosphere are actively regulated by the sum of life on the planet: the **biota**. This regulation of the Earth's surface by and for **biota** has existed continuously since the first appearance of life in an extensive manner. The guarantee of continued global habitability is, according to the Gaia hypothesis, not merely a matter of chance. The Gaian view of the atmosphere constitutes a radical detour from the early scientific concept that life on Earth is surrounded **by** and adapted **to** an essentially static environment. That life interacts with and ultimately transforms its own environment; that the atmosphere is an extension of the **biosphere** in almost the

---

[18] Id. **Ibid.**

116

same sense that the human mind is an extension of DNA; that life **interacts** with and **controls** the physical attributes of the Earth on a global scale, all of these things resonated strongly with the ancient magico-religious sentiment that all is one".[19]

The Gaian idea is simple: life is born and remakes its own environment, comes out of its self-absorption, and builds around itself a conducive cubicle, a thermal tent of breathable air, and slightly gradient climatic tuning forks. In this way, it controls the cosmic crises - ups and downs in solar radiation, the substitution of the initial reducing atmosphere by an oxidizing atmosphere - and, above all, thanks to microorganisms that "exhibit impressive capacities to transform the nitrogen, sulfide, and carbon contained in the gases in the atmosphere[20]", it builds on the surface of our planet a habitat regulated from within and not from outside the **ecosphere**.

The support of the thesis is rich and convincing. Gaian regulatory systems, similar to embryological ones as understood by Waddington, can be more adequately described as homeorhetic rather than homeostatic, and the final demonstration game, the computer simulation that supports this thesis, is based on the mathematical model Daisyworld. This model "has simple assumptions: the surface of the world hosts a population of living organisms comprising exclusively of black and white daisies. These organisms always reproduce properly. Each white daisy bears white daisies as fruit ["flowers" should have been used here] and each black daisy produces only daisies of its kind. All-black daisies absorb all the

---

[19] Dorian Sagan y Lynn Margulis, La hipótesis de Gea y la filosofía, en Leroy S. Rouner (comp.) **Sobre la Naturaleza**. Fondo de Cultura Económica, México, 1989.

[20] Conrad H. Waddington, resumen final del libro **Evolution and Consciousness**, compilado por él mismo y Erich Jantsch, Addison Wesley, Reading, 1976. Citado por Sagan y Margulis, **Op. cit**.

light that reaches them from the Sun and all-white daisies reflect all the light. It is considered that the best temperatures for the growth of both dark and light daisies are the same: they do not grow below a temperature of less than 5 degrees Celsius, increasing growth as a function of temperature to an optimum of 20 degrees and decreasing the rate of growth above the maximum of 40 degrees, at which temperature all growth ceases. Nevertheless, it is already clear that the **biosphere** acts as a supportive and sensitive organism, thanks to a surprising management of the composition of the reactive atmospheric gases. Here the triggering role of photosynthesis takes on a leading role, fighting against the increase of carbon dioxide and giving rise to a process that transforms it into deposits of calcium carbonate, which solidifies it in the bones of the skeletal frameworks or in the chitinous coverings that finally stow it in the white coral gardens or the black tombs of anthracite, the former sub-oceanic and the latter subterranean. Corals and coals are, after all, alchemical laboratory dumps and terminal deposits of biogenic matter.

If at present, we are terrified by the increase in carbon dioxide - the cause of the famous "greenhouse effect" caused by technological activity - we must understand that this imbalance imposed by man has broken the wise management that the Great Animal of the World had established from the depths of the evo. And ultimately, it makes us responsible for the ecocide of a biosphere of which we are part of and whose life, which is our own, we must preserve, if not lovingly, at least intelligently.

THE SNAIL OF LIFE

I am interested in snails. Actually, they summon both the attentive gaze of the naturalist and the third eye of the historian of the rituals of archaic and archaizing cultures. The snails not only represent the renewing forces of life that inhabit the subterranean domains where the terrestrial, chthonic divinities reign; they also carry the distinctive sign of the celestial gods: the spiral, key, and door of the uranic dynamism.

My encounter and colloquy with their signs and symbols come from far away, from my already remote childhood in the city of Paysandú. And what I narrate below, from an episode in the depths of my house, confirms the dark fraternity that unites me with these invertebrate mysteries.

SPRINGTIME IN THE GARDEN

The rain has stopped, and that is the signal for me to return to the garden. The downpour, which resounded reciprocally for half an hour over the roofs and the grove, prolongs the rumor of its passage in the fresh dripping that trickles down the foliage and falls on the dead leaves and the rustic flagstones, now turned into precious stones as they show, under the dust of the days washed by the torrent, the glow of their mica and quartz entrails.

Everything looks new and newborn. The colors of the leaves are clean and raw, and the nervation, sculpted rather than drawn, seem to have come out of the workshop of an artisan. There in the background, crowning the waters of the cycad, a gymnosperm surviving from the primary era, the branches of the laurel tree burn as if each one of them hid behind its matter a lamp of bloody light. From the bark of the dragon tree from the Canary Islands, from the avocados of the hot earth and the pitangas of the aboriginal flora, from the fleshy stems of the mantle of Eve, from the moss that fills the joints of the bricks, and above all, from the jasmine dressed as if for a party, a sweet scent comes forth, mingling with the almost acrid mist that rises from the soaked roots. A prolonged tremor, a humid shiver runs through the community of trees, bushes, and grasses whose intimate landscape, similar to that of the Japanese parks honeycombed in small spaces, seems to me a domestic fragment of that parade of the origins. Paradise, in Iranian, meant enclosed garden, because that, and nothing else was the plot of land that its creator and planter, The Great Gardener, gave to the care of the primordial couple.

I squat at the foot of the avocado trees, which in my long Colombian residence I learned to call avocados, a name in the Nahuatl language spread from its Mexican cradle throughout the tropical area of America. Ahuacatl means testicle, perhaps because of the shape of the fruit, perhaps because of the presumed aphrodisiac power of its oily pulp. My shoulders and hair get wet with a fine drizzle that intensifies at the slightest breath of wind, but that does not discourage me because something attracts and captivates my attention. I have seen the first snails and I want to contemplate closely to those golden and gibbous creatures with the old delight of my childhood in Sanducía, which I spent in the big house of Cerrito and Florida streets when in the middle of summer I used to collect them every two weeks to supply the stews of the blonde Alejandrina, the grandmother of the pots and pans.

LIKE THE TWO-FACED FACE OF NATURE

On the smooth, recently whitewashed wall, a pair of *He-lixPomatia* moves, undoubtedly descendants of the snails that, in full lethargy, arrived hidden among the agricultural seeds and equipment brought by the Spanish colonizers. One is massive, lustrous, with a thick shell, with purplish spots; the other is small, almost a snail project, covered with a pale shell, with translucent honey-colored edges. Both ascend laboriously, weighed down by the weight of the dwelling, a petrified and tiny galaxy with calcium spires manufactured by the internal alchemy of their bodies. Each of them leaves behind a trail of mucus that I am reluctant to call by its name. In the games of the light that reappears and is eclipsed again by the sun, that plays hide-and-seek with the last storm clouds, that mucus, instead of being a repellent and sticky substance, pretends to be woven - or is it really woven? - with the silver thread that sparkles in the stars, with the delicate silk that covers the viscera of the world.

The warmth of spring and the first fruits of the recently fallen rain have awakened and set in motion the society of snails, tender and at the same time solid mollusks like the two-faced face of Nature. I imagine them down there, in a slow collective awakening, unsheathing one after another the hollow turrets of those extravagant appendages celebrated by the dancing songs that the children, a Freemasonry that preserves millenary rites, still repeat in the swaying of their games: snail-eil-eil, / take out your horns for the sun /, that they come to kill you / at the seashore. [Children song]

The two early risers I have just discovered climb with choppy pace; they advance a few centimeters and then stop, perhaps to shake off the winter cold that has stuck to their transparent giraffe necks from the depths. Retreating inside their shells, they have spent the months of the bad season behind a calcareous operculum secreted by their organisms. This operculum, while sealing the shell, allows outside air access to the only lung that oxygenates land snails. But as the strategy of survival is more than just foresight, between the operculum and the body it has interposed a series of membranes, built by the gastropod in its escape into the shell, which prevents the entry of destructive agents and protects, like very thin gates, the vegetative confinement of the animal.

Naturalists, and after all I have had to learn their taxonomies and nomenclatures since the anthropologist is not a complete anthropologist if he does not deploy his flight from the ecosystems, classify snails within the Mollusca genus (from mollis, soft in Latin) and the *gastropoda* type, that is, with the foot in the belly, as it arises from the free translation of the Greek. The univalve, spiral shell of these homely specimens I am observing forces the fleshy mass to make a 180-degree twist around a counterclockwise axis. This sinistral arrangement, engraved in relief on the shell, represented the marine destruction that myths referred to as the negative powers of Poseidon. The whirlwind, oriented in this adverse way, had its replica in the creative spiral of Pallas Athena, dextrorotatory like the positive forces of the Kosmos, of the Order that supplants the Kaos and establishes a law between the elements of nature and the societies of men and gods. The Greeks, always dialectic, sought to establish in this way a system of counterweights, of harmonies, to escape the lurks of immoderation, the dreaded *hybris*.

The snails that inhabit the latitudes where the rhythmic pulsation of the seasons is fulfilled return with spring. They are indeed its emissaries, like the bears, to whom the man of the Paleolithic age, seeing them return from their winter sleep in the belly of the caves, attributed to them the virtue of bringing with them the restoration of life, and hence the traces of cultural ceremonies whose varieties are discovered today by archaeologists.

Depending on the mentality - sacred or profane - that interprets this advent, the snails, the bears, the dormice and the other sleepers of the animal kingdom resurrect or simply awaken. Confident in its knowledge of a "naturally" operated process, our Western rationality relegates mythical fables to the dark territories of superstition and primitivism. We no longer believe in the circularity of eternal returns, even if in itself the re-evolution, which, etymologically speaking, is after all the same thing. The unilinear progress, a dogma that sustains the religion of industrialism and scientism, is against the cyclical cosmogonic back and forth between the Kitra times and the Kali time, which Saint Simon renamed and transferred to the earth by calling them organic phases and critical phases of human society.

But what is certain and admitted by all is that when the snails reappear, they come with such a tremendous appetite that at the first onslaught they devour every appetizing vegetable that falls under their radulae, which is the name given to the rough horny tongues, efficient to the highest degree.

Between the Opposition and the Harmony of Opposites

I am interested, then, in snails. For what they are in themselves and for what we men have added, ideally, to their mere animal being. These horticultural gastropods not only represent the renewing forces of life that inhabit the subterranean domains where the terrestrial, chthonic, and therefore feminine divinities reign, to the point that, among the Aztecs, they symbolized the sequence that goes from conception to pregnancy and childbirth. They also carry the distinctive sign of the celestial gods, that is, the spiral, key, and door of the uranic dynamism that, from the medium sized, represented by the mass and dimensions of our planetary home, and the small sized, condensed in our bodies and our souls, fragments of matter and energy of the cosmic plasma.

Therefore, snails are strange hermaphroditic specimens whose reciprocal copulation makes each of the mating pairs simultaneously male and female. This may be of great interest to those who are on the hunt for new eroticisms and fantastic sensations, although the West, which has already surpassed the pleasures of Sodom and Gomorrah, is barely a gymnastic apprentice when compared to the sexology and sexonomy of India, China, and Japan.

To all of that, to the mythical and the biotic, I, for my part, have added the poetic. For a long time, I have been contemplating snails with that inquisitive passion that the reading of Henri Fabre's books transmitted to me in the distant days of my childhood: that is, with the enthusiasm of the poet, in the understanding that enthusiasm means nothing other than the inspiration granted by the gods to the human spirit where they provisionally dwell. And when the suffocated poet who is under my skin wants to manifest himself, I must restrain myself, warning myself that in my character of university *HerrProfessor* of such serious subjects as human ecology and comparative religions -the basement and the attic, respectively, of the house of anthropology- I must contemplate reality from a cold zone of thought, trying to understand and not to fabulate, giving way to the episteme and taking in all *poiesis*. That is why I must now strip the facts of all imaginative aura in order to stick to the scientific interpretation of the attributes granted by pre-literate cultures to those creatures that at this moment ascend towards neguentropy, leaving behind them the traces of cultured zooanthropic ancestors and the double wake of a frozen beauty.

Prehistoric burials reveal the frequent use of snails and shells to accompany human remains in tombs decorated, among other things, with shells of terrestrial and marine mollusks. The former have been collected locally, but the latter, those born in the *benthos*, come from very distant coasts, which suggests a bold and intense trade: man is such due to *sapiens* but also by *viator*.

Most of the archaic funerary snails belong to species contemporary to the burials. But some specimens, the ammonites, and nummulites, for example, are fossil testimonies of the secondary and tertiary eras.

Questions that Th. Meinage asked 70 years ago come to my mind: why did the skeleton of Laugerie-Basse (Dordogne) wear a necklace made of Mediterranean shells and the skeleton of Cro-Magnon an ornament of oceanic shells? Why is it that in the Grimaldi cave, Menton (Côte d'Azur), mortuary sites have provided shells from the shores of the Atlantic, while in Pont-à-Lesse (Belgium) fossil shells from the Tertiary period were found, collected in the area around Reims (France)?

The answers perhaps come from mechanisms that we cannot decipher with our logic, after all the daughter of the nominalism of the culture of the West, and not ubiquitous and eternal like the Platonic Ideas, supposedly real and valid for every place and every time.

However, for the prehistoric mentality (is there really such a thing as prehistory when only men can be the protagonist and at the same time the archive of all possible history, to such an extent that the word prehistory should mean the absence of humanity), the appeal to the distant object may have to do with the otherness of a vital force that must be renewed with the *hierophanies* of the opposite cardinal points or of the places possessing *mana*.

Thus, the Afterlife of the marine gastropods would be the here and now of the constant circulation of the genesic power, reanimator of plants and animals, of the beneficial stars, the Sun and the Moon, and also engenderer and midwife of newborns.

It is not possible to evoke, case by case, the magical occurrence of the snails in the customs of the people. The corpses were deposited on layers of snails or buried in the shells of the Sambaquian cultures scattered along the Atlantic coasts of Brazil, and the same happened on the African coasts. The sea snail was used by the Incas and the Aztecs, whose empires had their centers far away from the marine coasts, as a caller of the attention of the gods, and still today the moaning mooing of the mountain potutos, called fotutos in Colombia, my other homeland, prolongs the blowing of the oceanic wind among the snowy mountains.

Visitors to the prodigious Gold Museum in Santa Fe de Bogota can admire a fotuto made of thin sheets of tumbaga, the product of the remarkable metallurgy of the pre-Hispanic indigenous communities. Such a piece was not conceived, at

126

the time it was forged by the goldsmiths, as a pure manifestation of art but as an instrument of ritual. I make this noticeable,
as a plausible bridgehead for future wanderings on the path of
understandings and misunderstandings between the aesthetic
and the numinous.

The snail constituted, in short, a symbol of the fecundity
harbored in the waters of the sea and, at the same time, it
turned out to be the unanimous father of life in the traditions
of nuclear America, in the funeral ceremonies of Borneo and
in the burials of the Chinese desert of Fu-Chien. And it was
also the initial material of theogonies, one of which, the Hellenic one, inspired Thales of Miletus, who, changing *mythos*
for *logos*, conferred on the water the character of the primordial *arjé*.

THE LIFE THAT RETURNS WITHOUT PAUSE

The snail was used for buying and selling in the
slavedriver Africa and still circulates today among the tribes,
increasingly deculturated and degraded, where the
Cypraeamoneta serves as a vehicle for commercial transactions and as a ceremonial ornament. The disturbing drawing of
the shells of the snails is pampered in the Corsican dance of
the *caragola*, a choreographic spiral that the professional
weepers, today almost extinct, describe around the deceased
while they launch pitiful wails and shake their hair of ululating
Eumenides. The ancient Chinese urns of the Ma-Cheng period
also reproduce the incised motif of the snail spiral as an orna-
mental constant that, like a passport, assured the happy entrance to the Land of the Ancestors.

Why continue? The few examples above prove that the snail, the -Home- carrier, the *phereoikos* that springs from the newly dawning spring with its mineral flask on its back, "fleeing from the Pleiades" as Hesiod says, is one of the most useful symbols of the life that returns without pause. Its magical spiral mentions fecundity, the lunar theophany of the Aztec god Tecsiztecal, the maternal waters of the ocean, magical because of its mysterious remoteness, and the theocratic presence of the superhuman that binds death with life, immanence with transcendence, *atman* with *brahman*. When the Berber dancers of North Africa still today wave in their dances the shell necklaces that adorn the ceremonial masks, they try to transmit without words to those who contemplate them an ancestral message that, if decoded, would read as follows: "Here is the constant miracle of births, the humidity of the earth and of the sexes that smell of open furrow and spilled semen, the breath of the mouth of the dead that from the root of the sowing fields and the hospice of the tombs vitalizes us. All this strengthens our certainties and corroborates our sacred routines, thus helping us to maintain the order of the Universe and of society by achieving daily nourishment for ourselves and for our children".

While I think of these worlds and underworlds, thanks to an exercise of reverie closer to fantasy than to anthropology, the snails have disappeared. Unbeknownst to my chimeras, these living fragments of the domestic agro-system of my garden, which has ceased to be the free ecosystem of nature, will already be playing their role as primary consumers. Or perhaps they will have continued their exploration up the wall, parsimonious miniature monsters, hoisting the tentacles that communicate them, mythical antennae after all, with the realm of the immortals. These tentacles, strictly speaking, are four per individual. Two, very short and tactile, are oriented downwards. The other two, also tactile and contractile, are also optical and act as sensitive periscopes that retract at the slightest breath of breeze or at the cold passing of a shadow. Since both, the south wind and the threshold of the night already on top of things approach, I tell myself that it is time to retreat. An unpleasant sunset, like the ones we Uruguayans know, brings me back to the tasty conversations with my wife, to the smoky and aromatic red wine from Antioquia and the oriental cane with pitanga, to my current readings on the pre-Hispanic indigenous metallurgy, the Hellenic *polis,* and Hinayana Buddhism, to my nocturnal Mozart and Gardel, to the melancholic time machine that grinds memories in every corner of the house and without children, neat and empty. Before entering, a pampero breath promotes a whirlwind of leaves, half dry, half wet, which manufactures with its aerial winch an ephemeral sonorous snail. And up there, among the branches of the trees, resounds once again the bitter and assorted lament of those fotutos that for twelve years in a row blew on my Rioplatense nostalgia in the mineral building of the Andes.

But now, the Colombian mountains are the ones which, wind and time above, claim the memory of my divided heart.

www.ingramcontent.com/pod-product-compliance
Lightning Source LLC
Chambersburg PA
CBHW061353250726
48657CB00004B/1465